"California Dreaming is a touc... ....e Mountaintop Series, capturing the bittersweet shift from youth to adulthood. David Ferrier paints the '70s and '80s with warmth and clarity as Dave, Margaret Mary, and Teddy face choices that test friendships and shape their futures. It's a heartfelt reflection on change, connection, and the complicated beauty of growing up."

"California Dreaming is a nostalgic, emotional, and deeply human story that beautifully captures the uncertain stretch between youth and adulthood. I love the new book with Dave, Teddy and Margaret Mary."

"This book shines with its honest portrayal of personal growth, shifting dreams, and the bittersweet tension between connection and independence. I went back to thinking of where I came from and where I was headed at this age."

I really love this series. Great characters in the backdrop of California in the early 1980s, it feels authentic and has just the right amount of nostalgia. Perfect as a summer read, and just a very personal and human journey. I highly recommend reading the whole series.

CALIFORNIA DREAMING

David Ferrier

Battle Press
SATELLITE BEACH, FLORIDA

CALIFORNIA DREAMING

Copyright © 2025 by David Ferrier.

Battle Press books may be ordered through booksellers or by contacting:

Battle Press
1-919-218-4039
steve@battlepress.media
www.battlepress.media

ISBN: 979-8-9905619-6-0 (eBook)
ISBN: 979-8-9905619-7-7 (Paperback)
LCCN: 2025903763

First Edition.

OTHER BOOKS BY DAVID FERRIER

THE MOUNTAINTOP SERIES:

Born On A Mountaintop

Raised On Rock

Forged In Fire

Wired For Sound

After Your Military Service

A Cry For Mercy In The Night

Self Inflicted Wounds

.

Table Of Contents

Sing in Me Muse,
Of Choices Undertaken,
And Chances That are Wagered
As Lives Outlast the Legends.

Dedication:

To The Companions
Who Surround Me,
Nurture Me,
Encourage Me,
May Our Circle Be Unbroken.

The area dividing the brain and the soul
is affected in many ways by experience.

Some lose all MIND and become
INSANE

Some lose all SOUL and become
INTELLECTUAL

Some lose both and become
ACCEPTED

Charles Bukowski

Prologue

B eginnings, Middle and Ends.

Such are the trials and triumphs, efforts and failures of David, Margaret Mary, Teddy and all the rest as their lives flow on and paths must be chosen and followed.

In this collection of stories growing older corresponds with growing up for some, not so much for others. Effort, not outcome matters, and what counts for each one of us shifts as life moves forward.

Hopes and dreams, plans and schemes evolve, prosper and falter fueled by dreams and dreamers. The goals alter, geography changes, values shift but in the ideal, at least for some the value is in Dream in', California Dreamin'.

Chapter One

Beginnings, Middles & Ends

A few short days ago I was a slightly long in the tooth twenty-six-year-old college senior. Today I am unemployed, a college graduate, living at home with his parents, a failure to launch, near-do-well. Something had to change. Everything had to change.

After receiving my diploma from UMass I closed up my Squire Village apartment and left town on the same day that Richard Nixon skulked out of the White House one step ahead of the handcuffs, on August 9, 1974. Having more dignity than "Tricky Dick" wasn't much to congratulate myself for as I moved (temporarily, I hoped) back to Lowell and into my Glenmere Street childhood bedroom.

Less than a month later, while I was still trying to figure out what to do next, lifelong political hack and Nixon's handpicked successor as President of the United States, Gerald Ford, issued a full and unconditional pardon to The Trickster for "any crimes that he might have committed against the United States while President." Might have committed? What the hell?

Let Justice Prevail.

To make events even more ducky my current girlfriend, Emily Kazantoros, had begun working full time as a hostess at an upscale restaurant in Lowell where she was hit on regularly by doctors, lawyers and Indian chiefs. I couldn't blame them, she was very pretty, dressed stylishly and more and more available as I became more and more unemployable. I couldn't blame her, I was wavering between settling down and going "over the hill and far away," wherever and whatever that was. Local job opportunities were somewhat limited and none-what interesting.

I applied for a job with the Massachusetts State Police and was turned down. I briefly considered re-enlisting in the Army but came to my senses just in time. Teddy assured me I could follow him into the Lowell Police Department but, truth be told, I was shed, in my mind, of the old hometown and wanted to wander.

There was the whole Border Patrol opportunity from college. Both former Roomie Ron and I had received letters of acceptance into the Border Patrol a few weeks ago but Ron confided in me that he wasn't going to attend the Border Patrol Academy in October as we had planned. He asked me not to say anything to his father until he had a chance to tell him. I wasn't fully committed myself, but the Border Patrol was an open option, "over the hill and far away."

"I only want to know if we have a future together," Emmy said as we sat outside her house late one summer night.

Which started me into a now familiar stutter and stammer routine. I truly didn't know, couldn't decide. Up to now my future had always been just get through the day, one day at a time. It was a habit I learned in Nam. Don't worry about what's going to happen tomorrow, stay focused on what's happening today. Worked fine in Phu Bai, even worked pretty well in Amherst, not so much in Lowell. Not so much with Emmy.

She was a keeper, no doubt about it. I enjoyed her company. She enjoyed mine. But a future? I was having trouble with that, not her, that.

So far, the most exciting, vivid, essential, challenging and worthwhile part of my life had been flying Dustoff in Vietnam. Yes, it was dangerous. Youth serves. Realistically it was a nightmare, the whole war, a soul-scorching, a national disgrace on the political level. But in-country, day to day, alongside my fellow soldiers, it was the most rewarding and inspiring thing I had ever done. I was part of a team of the most courageous men I ever knew. I had a purpose. I was part of something larger than myself, an effort to do good, to be good. I wanted more of that and couldn't find it anywhere in the tiny, inconsequential world I returned to.

"I'm having a lot of trouble with the whole 'future' thing, Em." I began, "Not you, I love you, but I don't know what I'm going to do with myself. I have no job, very few prospects and no real plan. I don't feel like I'm part of anything here anymore. I feel like I'm less than I was, and if I stay around here, I'll be less than I could be. You deserve a home and a family and a lifestyle I don't think I can provide. At least not here, not now."

"Are we breaking up?" She asked quietly.

"I'm going to give the Border Patrol a chance, Em. It means moving to Texas, there's a sixteen-week Academy and then an assignment somewhere along the Texas/Mexico border."

"I don't think I want to live in Texas," Emmy said sadly.

"And I don't want to stay in Lowell," I replied. So, after a hug and a few tears and promises to stay in touch we said goodnight and goodbye. Texas, here I come.

On my ride home from Emmy's that night the radio whispered, and I hoped I wouldn't hear the voice of Roy Orbison, who, right on cue, sang...

If heartaches brought fame in love's crazy game,

I'd be a legend in my time.

If they gave gold statuettes for tears and regrets,

I'd be a legend in my time. *

I turned the damn radio off and drove home.

"This one, this artist, I can feel his work," Aunt Rose pronounced as she and Sean toured La Premiere Expression II and Margaret Mary and Gianna proudly showed off their studio.

"This is Jean Michael Tousignant. He lives here, in Paris, with five cats and a very nervous canary," Gianna laughed as she explained. "Jean has four paintings with us now. We have sold three others. He comes by every week, on Wednesday, to have lunch with us. I think he is hopelessly in love with Margaret Mary, as we are hopelessly in love with his work."

Sean had wandered over to the wall which displayed the work of the Gaelic artists Margaret Mary had discovered and showcased from Dublin.

"These are beautiful," He said. "I think it is very important that you give them this exposure. Do they sell?"

"Oh, Father, a chancellor from Notre Dame University bought three, three of the best, to take back to Indiana where they will hang in the Administration building!" Margaret Mary beamed.

"His wife bought another for their personal collection and a Tousignant as well," Gianna added. "We also have offers on these two and your very discerning daughter will be returning to Dublin soon to buy several more."

"I am also going to see works in Kilkenny and Cork. Perhaps we can all go together!" Margaret Mary proposed.

"Perhaps we shall," Rose answered. "However, I believe there was some mention of dinner? Three little pigs, if I recall?"

"Aux Tres Petits Cochons," Margaret Mary laughed in her ever-improving Francais. "It is only right around the corner; we can walk there!"

Which they did, arm in arm in arm in arm.

Happy.

Kevin sat at the bus stop on a rainy Tuesday morning staring at his hands. He was reluctant to get a driver's license and rode the Centerville bus to the YMCA every morning, save Sunday. He lived at home with his mother and did not go out to any degree other than to and from work. He fostered no friends other than the kids who came to the gym to box and felt strong emotion only when he held his niece, Samantha, during his frequent, but brief visits to Teddy and Beth's home. Kevin was not unhappy, he was not joyful, he was somewhere within himself, safe.

"Duck, duck, duck and dodge, then jab!" Kevin encouraged the young fighter, pleased at the effort, if not the result. Work was his refuge, his muse, his reason for rising and resting each day. He felt only the dim satisfaction of seeing progress in his students, their self-confidence growing as his did not, their faces smiling as his could not.

"That kid keeps dropping his left he's gonna' get clobbered," Teddy observed as he entered the gym.

Kevin turned to see Teddy, in his full police uniform, walking toward the heavy bag. Teddy gave it a half-hearted poke and shuffled past.

"Can you go by the house tonight on your way home?" Teddy muttered, "I gotta' work a double and I don't want Beth to be left alone all that time with the kid."

"The kid" was how Teddy had come to refer to his daughter. His disabled, crippled, cheerful, beautiful daughter he could barely look at anymore. When he was not feeling at fault for Samantha's condition, he was feeling sorry for himself, or angry with everything and everybody else. The sorrow he felt for Samantha became the pain he wallowed in every day. Even Kevin, behind his high walls of safety, noticed.

"You shouldn't call her that," Kevin chided. "Her name is Samantha."

"Don't you worry about what I call my own kid. If you don't wanna' go by, don't." Teddy turned to leave.

"I'll go by," Kevin said to Teddy's back. Teddy didn't stop walking. Kevin clenched his fists, anger seeping through his half light, then fading. He turned back to the gym and went about his morning.

"Duck, dodge and jab," he intoned to the young fighter, "and keep you're left up. You're gonna' get clobbered if you don't."

As they all were.

The Oakland California Police Dispatch sent the following message to a patrol car on Saturday night, September 14th, 1974.

"Unit 417 respond to the alley behind the Tic Toc Lounge. There is a report of a body in a dumpster."

"Tic Toc's that biker bar over on Stuart," the driver said as he turned the cruiser around.

"Night wouldn't be complete without a visit to a biker bar," His partner said as they rolled to the call.

When officers Terry Mealick and Lucius Taylor arrived at the Tic Toc they found Tommy Watts, the bar's manager, in the alley. He was leaning against the lounge door smoking a cigarette. This was not his first body in a dumpster.

"Over there," he pointed, "Bar back found it when he was dumpin' the trash."

Lucius Taylor got out of the car and crossed to the dumpster. He peered in and saw the bruised and battered body of a Caucasian male, mid-twenties, maybe thirty.

"Call for the meat wagon," Lucius said, "I ain't goin' in there after him."

Thirty minutes later the corpse was laid out on a stretcher next to the ambulance. The victim was very dead, badly beaten, all his pockets were turned inside out and he only had one arm. Tommy Watts wandered over and looked at the body.

"That's Flipper," he said. "That's what they called him anyway. Ken something, nah, it was Kendall. Came into the bar every now and then. Looks like he shoulda' stayed away."

"You got any idea who might have done this?" Lucius asked, knowing the answer.

"Who me? I ain't got no ideas about nuthin'. You done with me?"

Lucius nodded and Tommy went back into the bar. "Take him to the morgue. Book him in as John Doe until the prints come back."

The ambulance attendants packed up the body and left. Lucius and Terry got another call from dispatch. Flipper was headed for the morgue.

Kendall Prescott, malevolent guru of the Tuloc Meadow commune, rapist, kidnapper and asshole now known only as Flipper, was no more.

Fuck him.

I was leaving for Texas, Margaret Mary was leaving for Dublin, Teddy was leaving fatherhood, and "Flipper" left the planet.

A Beatle named George, who was no longer a Beatle, sang a eulogy…

Sunrise doesn't last all morning,
A cloudburst doesn't last all day,

Seems my love is up and left you with no warning,
It's not always going to be this way.

All Things Must Pass,
All Things Must Pass Away. **

And many, if not all of my things were passing.

Lyrical Aspirations:
*I'd Be A Legend In My Time, Ronnie Milsap
**All Things Must Pass, George Harrison

Chapter Two

The Day The Music Died

The morning newscast hit Teddy hard. Four large shots of bourbon hard, all before 10 AM. He was too drunk to go to work, too drunk to walk a straight line, too drunk to keep himself from crying. He collapsed onto his living room sofa and stared blindly at the morning news program flickering from the TV. Beth heard her husband sobbing and came into the room carrying Samantha. She looked at the TV, moaned "Oh my God!" and took a seat on the sofa next to her inconsolable husband.

Gruesome, ghostly images of clanking tanks on city streets, burning buildings, grim soldiers terrorizing panicked civilians, flickered on the TV screen.

Beth took Teddy's hand, he pulled it away, rose and stormed into the bedroom, slamming the door behind him. His sobs grew louder. The tanks clanked on.

"Mon Dieu! C'est terrible! Mon pauvre David!"

Margaret Mary had come to expressing herself in Francais as often as in English as her time in Paris went on. She sat transfixed as their seldom used but always present television broadcasted the disturbing news. Flickering images of buildings aflame, panicked crowds, rumbling tanks on city streets and chaos filled the air.

"What is it? What has happened?" Gianna asked, rushing into the room. She stopped as the TV answered her question. She sat next to Margaret Mary, took her hand. "Your David, he was there?"

Margaret Mary could only nod, her eyes filled with tears. The TV news groaned silently on.

"This is an abomination, a stain on our Nation's integrity. A catastrophe," Horatio Marks muttered while watching his office television. The tragic story was being covered nationwide, on every channel, all morning long.

Peter Rayburn and Cindy Cassen were also in Horatio's office, stunned by what they were seeing.

"This is going to be awfully hard on your friend Dave," Cindy offered.

"Awfully hard on a lot of people, but especially guys like Dave," Horatio replied.

"Imagine how the families must feel," Peter mused aloud. "The families of all those who died there."

Silence prevailed. Shame descended. The broadcast went on.

The news from "down below" usually took its time getting to Hume, Alaska. Here the weather to come, the fish to gather and the friendships to be nurtured made up the majority of the news the locals responded to. But not today. Bad news is swift. This news was the swiftest.

LT didn't own a TV. He arrived at the American Legion lodge around noon to have lunch and coffee with his friend and Alaska State Trooper Luke Drayber. LT came in, waved to the barman and took a seat at a table, back to the bar.

Luke Drayber was grim, looking over LT's shoulder at the wall mounted TV behind the bar.

"LT, you should see this," He said sadly.

LT turned to see a UH-1H American helicopter being pushed off the landing deck of the USS Hancock. The chopper's rotor blades were still turning when it hit the sea and exploded. Terrified, crying, huddled groups of Vietnamese refugees were being herded below decks. Another chopper approached. It lost altitude and crashed into the sea. Rescue boats were launched.

"What the hell is going on?' LT demanded.

"Saigon's fallen. We're pulling our people out. These are the last of them." Luke Drayber realized his words were cutting LT to pieces.

Pulling out? Retreating? Abandoning the country? Losing the war? LT tried to process his thoughts, smother his anger, control his memories. He was speechless.

Other townsfolk wandered into the lodge. They looked ashamed. The ones who knew LT, and most of the town did, looked at him with sorrow, with pity. LT didn't notice. He was far away, remembering Lance Corporal Jesus Ortega bleeding to death in a rice paddy outside Da Nang. He remembered the young corporal's eyes pleading, his last words stammering, "Tell me Madre, tell me Madre…" And he died before he could finish the sentence.

Two days later when LT led his men back to the firebase he wrote a letter to Lance Corporal Ortega's mother. He told her her son died bravely, that he was a good Marine and that he had died helping the people of South Vietnam fight the Communists. He told her she could be proud of her son. LT remembered every word of the letter he had written and others just like it. Today he could not remember or reason what any of those men had died for. He stopped looking at the TV.

That morning, I arrived at the Sierra Blanca Border Patrol station to start my shift. I was seven months into my career as a United States Border Patrolman. After a lot of all-too-familiar procrastination I decided to leave Lowell, break off my relationship with Emmy Kazantoros and give Texas a try. So far, so good. But only so far. Things were about to change.

The first four months in the Patrol were at the Federal Law Enforcement Academy in Los Fresnos, Texas. It was sort of like Army boot camp with lots of textbooks. We learned Immigration Law, Tex/Mex Spanish, Code of Conduct for Federal Officers, Tactics and Maneuvers, Defensive Driving and Weapons Proficiency, plus lots and lots of push-ups, five mile runs and, best of all, for me, boxing and self defense.

I attended the Academy without Roomie Ron, who, despite my best efforts and his father's juice, eloped to Florida with his no longer almost fiancé a week before we were scheduled to report for training.

The Academy was rigorous and demanding. About two hundred candidates started training. A little over a hundred of us finished. I had a blast. The training cadre respected veterans, such as myself, and those of us with military backgrounds tried to pass along what we knew to the other candidates.

"They are doing this for us, not to us," We tried to explain. All the yelling, cursing, criticizing, grunting and groaning was meant to toughen us up, get us ready for life on the border, carrying guns, dealing with gunmen. Some listened, many quit. I graduated high in the class. I worked hard to do that. It felt good, familiar. Back in the saddle again. The Texas/Mexico border wasn't Phu Bai, but it would do. For now.

Until now.

A small black & white TV in the corner of the squad room displayed ghostly images of overloaded helicopters lifting off Saigon rooftops with desperate people clinging to their skids. I clocked in and wandered over to where several other Patrolmen were watching the TV. I saw sailors pushing helicopters over the side of their ships into the South China Sea. I saw a North Vietnamese tank dragging a burning American flag through the streets of Saigon. Then a talking head in a gray suit came to a podium in Washington D.C. and solemnly announced that all remaining US ground and support troops had been withdrawn from South Vietnam and that the North Vietnamese forces now controlled the country.

My knees actually became weak, and tears filled my eyes. Dan Sorenson, one of my new Border Patrol buddies who I knew to have been an infantry sergeant in the 101st Airborne, looked like he was crying as well. I spun around and kicked a defenseless folding chair across the office. This got the attention of Gordon Barnes, our Senior Patrol Officer. He came out of his office, glared at me, glanced at the TV and ordered me, and Dan Sorenson into his office. He took his place behind his desk, folded his hands in front of him and said, "I've seen the news. I know both of you served in Vietnam. This is not a day for our country to be proud of, but I want you to know I am proud of both of you. I want you both to take the day off. Do what you need to do to deal with this. The disgrace is not yours."

Then Dan said something I have always wished I said, "With all due respect sir, I'd like to stay on duty today. Of all days, today is one where I want to know I did my duty just like I did in Nam. I want to stay on the job for all the guys I served with who can't."

I nodded a meek and sorrowful, "Me too." We left Barnes' office. The TV was chuckling over the latest news from Hollywood. It was going to be a long, long, day remembering a long, long war. I could find no song in my heart or melody in my head to dull this pain as ghostly voices whispered in my ear…

"Let every nation know, whether it wishes us well or ill, that we shall pay any price, bear any burden, meet any hardship, support any friend, oppose any foe, to assure the survival and success of liberty."

John Fitzgerald Kennedy, 35th President of the United States January 20, 1961.

"I am not going to be the first American President to lose a war."

Richard Milhouse Nixon, 37th President of the United States, November 10, 1969

"Today Americans can regain the sense of pride that existed before Vietnam."

Gerald Ford, 38th President of the Untied States, April 23, 1975.

April 30, 1975, The day our National Anthem Died.

Chapter Three

Rivertime

Darkness is what you see. Movement is what you notice. Silence is what you hear.

Rolling on the river, Texas/Mexico border. August 1975.

I was perched above a dry wash that ran north from the Rio Grande River for about four miles, then rose to the high desert plain close to the Interstate Freeway outside of Sierra Blanca, Texas. It was around three in the morning, maybe a little later. A waning moon cast a silvery light into the shadows.

Six figures were walking up the wash. Four were carrying heavy backpacks. Two had rifles. One rifleman walked ahead of the group, the other behind. They were approaching a blacked-out panel van parked on the slope leading from the wash. A driver sat in the van, smoking, waiting. He had not seen the group approaching yet.

I had been watching the van for over two hours. My partner, Dan Sorenson, was behind the walkers, keeping low and out of sight. The van driver heard a noise and looked up. The lead rifleman signaled. The van driver blinked the van's headlights twice. The group arrived at the van. There was some low muttering in Spanish and the four men with backpacks dropped their burdens to the ground. The side panel of the van slid open, and the rear rifleman motioned for the four men to load their packs into the van.

When that was done, they would either all climb into the van and leave, or the rifleman would kill the four walkers and leave in the van with the packs. I didn't wait to find out which.

I sparked a highway flare and threw it into the wash. My partner, Dan, threw another. Eerie red light flickered in the gully. The rifleman looked around for targets.

"Manos Arriba!" I shouted and for emphasis I blew out the right front tire of the van with my Remington Pump shotgun. Dan pumped a round into the air from behind the group and added, "Manos Arriba Pronto!"

Then I blew out the left front tire of the van. The riflemen hesitated, searching for us in the darkness. Dan fired another round into the air and shouted, "Vamos! Tira el arma, pronto!"

The riflemen decided to give it up. They laid their rifles down on the ground. The four walkers crouched in terror. The van driver lit another cigarette.

"Baja al suelo ahora!" I shouted, working out my Spanish chops. "Pon tus manos entu cabeza!"

Now that Dan and I had them safely on the ground with their hands on their heads we each threw another flare into the wash and stepped out of the darkness, guns up. I gathered the grounded rifles. Both were lever action Marlin repeaters, 30.30's. They looked brand new.

Dan cuffed the riflemen, and I shook down the driver. He had a Colt 1902 hammerless pistola in his belt. I cuffed him and set him down with the rifleman. The four walkers looked terrified. None were carrying weapons. Their backpacks each held about sixty pounds of tightly packaged marijuana, Mexican brown. Each had a large black scorpion stenciled on the package. Cartel packages. The four walkers had a small bandanna of personal belongings tied to their waist. Dan collected these and tossed them into the back of the van.

"I'll call for the cage and a tow truck," I said as I climbed out of the wash to where my prowler was parked. Dan kept his shotgun on the group of men.

"Grant's going to be pissed off," Dan said as I turned to leave.

"Better to be pissed off than pissed on," I replied and made the calls.

I felt good, satisfied, energized, restored. I still couldn't believe I got paid to do this stuff.

Teddy had taken to hiding a pint of Popov vodka under the front seat of his patrol car. Most days the pint would last all day. He would buy another on his way home from work. This one he hid in the bathroom, under the sink, in the far corner of the cabinet. It too would be empty by morning.

Teddy drank when he saw his daughter, Samantha, squirming in her crib, her twisted spine giving her discomfort. He drank when his wife Beth cradled the child and looked at him with an expression he interpreted as being, "This is all your fault." Beth meant her expression to convey, "It's going to be alright, don't worry so." Teddy drank anyway, incorrectly and often.

He drank when he remembered pulling a dead comrade through the mud of Vietnam to a landing zone. He drank when he recalled helicopters being pushed into the ocean from the decks of fleeing ships. More and more he drank when he saw the endless cycle of poverty, crime, greed and foolishness on the streets of Lowell every day. He drank mornings and he drank nights, and it didn't help.

"Gianoulous, you are late, your uniform is slovenly, and this is the last time I am going to tell you to get a haircut." Commander Patrick Upson was a fair man, a good cop and a friend and supporter of his fellow officers. But his patience with Teddy was running short. Pat was a former Marine and understood the bond of "Semper Fi." Teddy was forgetting it.

"Yes sir," Teddy answered tucking in his uniform shirt. "Fuck you" he muttered as roll call ended. The kids that trained at the YMCA gym with his brother-in-law, Kevin, called Teddy "Officer Shit-faced" behind his back after several bleary visits to the gym. Kevin had reluctantly asked Teddy not to stop by when he had been drinking. He told Teddy the kids could smell the alcohol on him and so could he. Teddy left in a huff and hadn't been back in weeks.

The road to hell was getting steeper and slipperier for Teddy. He didn't much care.

"You two are becoming quite wealthy young women," Gianna's sister, Lucia, announced as they went over the books for La Premiere Impression II.

"Really? How wealthy are we?" Gianna asked.

"Wealthy enough to move from your tiny apartment. You two should think about buying a house, a home."

Gianna and Margaret Mary exchanged surprised expressions. Their gallery had been open a little over a year. Their early success continued. They loved their work. They loved each other. Perhaps it was time to look for a home.

"Are we then to be married?" Gianna asked later as she and Margaret Mary sat sipping espresso in a small café.

"I don't want to be a husband!" Margaret Mary laughed.

"Nor do I," Gianna agreed, smiling. "But wife and wife, it is difficult."

"Perhaps one day this will change," Margaret Mary replied.

"Perhaps one day we will change," Gianna said.

"I hope not," Margaret Mary answered. "I hope we can always be the same."

Hopeless as that was.

"You still driving the cab?" Eddie's probation officer asked.

"Yes sir," he answered as respectfully as he could manage.

"How many hours a week?"

"Forty, sometimes fifty."

"You got pay stubs?"

Eddie placed them on the officer's desk. The probation officer barely looked at them. "Good. Gimme the Pats and the points against Houston, the Jets straight up over San Diego, I'll take the under with Pittsburgh and the Bears. A hundred each."

Eddie scratched notes on his pad, counted the three hundred bucks and placed it in an envelope.

"See ya' next week," The probation officer said. Eddie left his office.

Let Justice Prevail.

"We registered thirty-four new veterans at the Loch Raven Medical Center. Twenty-two at Glen Burnie," Cindy reported as Peter made notes, and Horatio Marks tallied the figures.

"That's still not enough for the class action suit we want to file. We've got to figure a way to get more vets to file for disability based on exposure to Agent Orange," Horatio added.

"Los Angeles has close to three hundred, San Diego two hundred, we're getting there," Peter figured.

Both Peter and Cindy had finished their classwork at Suffolk University six months ahead of their classmates. They had taken the Massachusetts State Bar Exam three weeks earlier and were signed up for the Maryland Bar Exam in two weeks. There were no results in as yet for the Massachusetts exam, but Cindy was a 3-1 favorite to outscore Peter. Peter grinned like a wolf and bet on himself.

Peter and Cindy were still commuting between Boston and Baltimore but were spending much more time in Horatio's office these days. After meeting with Teddy, Beth and Samantha, Horatio had devoted much of his practice to veteran's disabilities, particularly the growing awareness of the horrific aftermath of Agent Orange exposure among Vietnam vets. Peter and Cindy had signed on, a worthwhile work in progress.

Nationwide there was a growing awareness of the Agent Orange tragedy. Peter and Cindy had agreed to take the case back to Massachusetts, recruiting veterans there for the lawsuit as well.

"Get in here Agent Ferrier and bring Sorenson with you." Our station Senior Agent, Gorden Barnes, was pissed. Just like we knew he would be.

"What the hell was that all about last night?" He growled as we stood, not at ease in front of his desk.

"Pack train sir," I replied, "Two coyotes, four mules, lots of dope."

"I know that. What I do not know is what you two were doing six miles off the Interstate in the tall and uncut and not at the checkpoint I assigned you to." Senior Agent Barnes was not calming down.

"Lopez was the driver sir. He tipped me at the checkpoint when he came through in the van. He couldn't say anything because he had a woman with him. I followed him into town. He dropped her off and headed east. I called Dan for backup and followed him."

"Lopez led you to the pickup?"

"He did sir," Dan Sorenson added.

"And what is this station's policy regarding suspected narcotics movements?"

"Four-man teams sir," I answered respectfully.

"And?" Barnes asked, knowing we had no good answer.

"No time sir," I ventured. "We would have had to shut the checkpoint down. I didn't want to use the radios in case they were monitored. I figured Dan and I could handle it."

"You figured." Barnes said, "Agent Ferrier you are still a probationary agent. You will be until you have a full year on the job. You are not authorized to 'figure.' You are authorized to follow orders."

"Yes sir," I replied, trying to look humble.

"Dan, you've got more sense than this. An agent was shot in Marfa three days ago. The gunman was using a Marlin 30:30, same as the two you picked up last night. The cartel is not handing those out as walking sticks. No more of this cowboy shit. Four-man teams, got it?"

Dan nodded respectfully. I continued staring at my shoes. That wasn't good enough for Barnes.

"I said, have you got it, Agent Ferrier?"

There is a time to say yes and then keep your mouth shut. This wasn't one of those times.

"Sir, with all due respect, if Dan and I hadn't followed Lopez there would probably be four dead dope mules in that ditch and a shitload of drugs on the way to the city."

"I don't care five cents worth about four dead dope mules! I do care about two dead Border Patrolmen! The drugs we can't help, it's a river. Let Customs handle it. From this point on, four-man teams, or you don't reach the end of your probation! Got it now?"

I did, I said so and we got the hell out of his office. Just like the old days.

Chapter Four

Epiphany, Epiphanies

Six weeks after rolling on the river I was strolling down a busy city street in El Paso, Texas. It was a bright, sunny Monday afternoon. I had on my Tony Llama boots, crisp, clean Border Patrol Green Uniform, rough duty hat with bad ass flattened brim and mirrored sunglasses. Oh, yeah, and a .357 Magnum, Ruger revolver, cuffs, keys and ammo hanging from my shiny black leather gun belt. Coincidentally I was carrying a 12-gauge Remington pump shotgun and a "don't fuck with me" attitude. I wasn't looking for trouble, I was trouble. Walking down the mid-day street in El Paso, Texas.

I had been called into Regional Border Patrol headquarters to face my final probationary review. After this I would be a full-on, no holds barred Patrolman. I wasn't worried. My record was good, I got along with my bosses, and I liked the work. Maybe a little too much.

An hour or so later I was back on the street. Armed, dangerous and no longer on probation. I added a swagger to my step as I walked back to my patrol car. Then I caught a look at myself in the mirrored glass of a store front. What I saw stunned me. The man in the mirror was not my friend. Looking back at me was a guy I wasn't at all sure I liked or wanted to be. Bad ass hat and all, I looked like a Nazi. Not a German, "Heil Hitler" Nazi, an American Nazi. The type of cop you just know is going to be an asshole.

In those increasingly fleeting moments when I was truthful with myself, I had come to realize that I was changing, and not for the good. I liked the guns, the gunfire, the "sneakin and creepin'" of the Texas/Mexico border. I asked to work midnight shifts, solo when possible, "mas peligroso," more dangerous, more fun, less rational. I was working nights, sleeping days and becoming a stranger to myself, and others.

I started to set myself apart from anyone in my life who wasn't Patrol, as many of the other men I served with have done. My world was becoming "Us" and the assholes. "Us" were Border Patrolmen, Cops, Texas Highway Patrol and Texas Rangers. Everybody else was an asshole. Such was my prevailing mindset as well as those of many of the men I worked with. This wasn't good. The man I saw in the mirror that Monday afternoon personified all I didn't want to be. I just stopped trying to not be that guy.

I had not spoken to Margaret Mary in months, several months. Neither had I spoken with my Father, my friends, anyone who wasn't one of "Us." I was once again apart, not in a good way, bad apart. When I saw my reflection in that glass, I realized I either had to change, and soon, or I would never change at all.

I had some serious decisions to make, and the answers were not inside my head.

"345 is, I believe, a higher score than 329, is it not?" Peter was not even trying to keep the smirk off his face or out of his voice.

Cindy fumed. Bar exam results were in. Passing score was 270. They were now both officially lawyers, at least in the state of Massachusetts. But Peter scored higher, 16 lousy points higher. She would never live this down.

"What I do not understand," Peter continued haughtily, "Is why, given these results, you still have any clothing on at all."

"Peter, I'm not in the mood."

"Must I refer you to the section regarding oral contracts?" Peter countered.

Cindy was trying very hard to remain indignant. But Peter's smirk, like Peter's beret, always brought out the best in her. She started undressing.

"Please come home Beth. I'm sorry."

"You're sorry when you're sober. How long are you going to be sober Teddy?" Beth replied.

Beth had been living with her mother and Kevin for two weeks. During that period Ted had tried to visit repeatedly. Kevin, or Gloria, turned him away. Today Teddy sat on their front porch and refused to go away until Beth spoke to him. Beth relented. Teddy confessed, "I haven't had a drink, not one, for a week, Beth, honest."

"Do you think the only reason I left you was because of your drinking?" Beth asked.

Teddy nodded, didn't answer, and stared at the ground, ashamed. Once again Beth relented.

"I left you because you cannot, or will not, or do not love our daughter," Beth said, herself overcome with shame. "You have made me sorry I married you, sorry you are my baby's father." Beth broke down in tears. Teddy did as well. Teddy took a step towards Beth. She backed away.

"Don't touch me!" She exclaimed. "The one you should be trying to hold, the one you should be crying for, is our daughter in the house. Until you can do that there is no us, do you understand?" Anger and determination replaced Beth's tears. Teddy stood frozen, choking on words he could not bring himself to say. Then, for the first time out loud, he sobbed, "It's my fault. I made her that way, it's my entire fault."

Before Beth could answer, before she could do anything, Teddy stormed away from the house into the night. His week of sobriety was over.

"David! I can't believe it's you! Why haven't you called me? I tried to call you; your Mother said you have no phone. I'm so happy to hear your voice!" Margaret Mary shouted into the phone.

"Mags, I'm in Texas, I don't think there are two people in the whole state who know how to place a trans-continental phone call and I'm not either one of them."

"But you called?"

"I found someone not from Texas to help me."

"No more joking! How are you? What are you doing? When will you come and see me? Tell me everything!"

The excitement in Margaret Mary's voice echoed the joy I felt in my heart at reaching her. For the first time in way too long I felt like me again, not one of the "Us" and I very much wanted to be who I was before the gun belts, the shotguns and the midnight shifts. As always Margaret Mary was the best place to start.

"I'm leaving Texas, Mags, resigning from the Border Patrol. It's not me, not the me I want to be anyway."

There was a silence on the phone. There was a silence in my head. That was the first time I ever said out loud I was leaving the Border Patrol. I had been thinking about it for weeks. Thinking hard. I hadn't really made up my mind until I heard Margaret Mary's voice. The silence continued, then Margaret Mary pronounced, "You must come see me right away. Please for me, for you. If I buy you a plane ticket, will you come here?"

I could hear the plea in her voice. "Mags, if I come to see you, I can buy my own plane ticket. I'm thinking of going back up to Lowell and kind of regroup."

"No! You must come here! You must! I have something to tell you, to ask you, and we must be together when I do. And you must see my beautiful Paris! Please, please, please, come here."

"Will I have to be sitting down when you tell me this thing?" I joked, referring to our past history of momentous announcements.

"David," she scolded, "What is more important for you to see? Lowell, again, or Paris and me!"

She had a very good point there. Leaving the Border Patrol and going back to Lowell would be just that, going backward. I didn't have a clue just yet of where I was going next but forward felt better than backward.

"What about your..." I couldn't bring myself to say girlfriend, "your friend, Josephine?"

"Her name is Gianna; you must not make jokes. She will be very happy to meet you. Please, please come."

"Okay," I heard myself saying. "I've got some things to do here, some logistics to figure out, but yes, I'll come. I'll call you when I have a schedule."

"Come soon, come quickly, I can't wait to see you!"

The joy that passed between us then was greater than words, or thoughts or feelings could convey. We babbled and gushed for several more minutes then hung up. I truly do not remember the end portion of our call, but two things were certain, I was going to Paris, and my Border Patrol career was over.

LT pulled into his driveway and was surprised to hear the sound of his kitchen telephone jangling. He had only had the phone installed a month ago and rarely, if ever, heard it ring. He hurried inside and answered to the sound of his mother's voice. "Robert, I need you to come home. It's your father, he's in the hospital. He is very ill."

One of LT's first calls when he had the phone installed had been to his parent's home. He called during the day when he knew his father would not be home. He spoke briefly with his mother, gave her the number before she ended the call, afraid her husband would return and be angry that she was speaking to her son.

"Mom, if Dad's ill and I show up it will only make him sicker."

"He can't get any sicker, Robert. He has decided to stop his chemotherapy. The doctor's say he will die within a week." LT heard the heartbreak in his mother's voice and felt a long buried pang of regret and sadness.

"Are you sure he wants me there?" LT asked, hopefully.

"Robert, I have spent the majority of my married life worrying about what your father wants and doesn't want. I want you here. Will you please come?"

And that settled the matter. LT was going home.

"What the hell are you doing here?" Lieutenant Colonel Robert Baker (Ret.) said as his son entered his hospital room.

"I'm here because you're sick Dad. Mom called me," LT replied.

"I'm not sick, I'm dying," The colonel growled. "Where's your mother?"

"She's out in the hall. She thought she would give us a moment alone." LT was already regretting he came.

"You still hiding up in Alaska?"

"I'm not hiding Dad, I live there."

"So you say."

"That's right, Dad, so I say. I live there, I have a good job, a home, I'm part of a community and if I'm hiding from anything, I'm hiding from you."

Which, for the very first time he could remember gave LT's father pause. Sad silence filled the room. LT got ready to leave.

"Hold on a minute, son, please."

LT froze in the door way. His father called him son. He said please. LT turned, his father continued, "I'm sorry I snapped at you. Dying people do that I suppose."

"You're dying because you want to Dad. Why are you stopping your treatment?"

"The chemo's not working any more, son. I have to come here three days a week now. I feel alright for maybe a day, then I get tired, and sick again. This is not going to get better."

LT knew this was true. He had talked with his father's doctor earlier. Multiple myeloma cancer was a fatal progression, it could be delayed, not cured.

"I have no quality of life left, son, not for me, not for your mother. It's best to end it now."

LT had no reply. He saw the frail, nearly helpless former Marine Corps Colonel hooked up to several machines, shrunken in the hospital bed and realized what he was saying was true.

"So what happens now?" LT asked.

"I go home, son. The medics tell me they can manage any pain and I will die in a few days."

LT let the words sink in. The tone in his father's voice was not anger, not command, it was sadness and regret.

"Would you sit down a minute, son. I'd like us to have that minute your mother gave us."

LT crossed to a chair, sat down. His father continued, "I'm sorry for the differences between us, son. I apologize for my behavior. My anger wasn't always at you, it was at myself and it was at what has happened to our country."

"It always felt like it was at me," LT replied.

"That Christmas when you came home all full of antagonism and spite, cursing out our President and that damned war, it was at you. Still, I was wrong and I'm sorry for what happened. I never should have hit you."

"Nixon was an asshole, Dad, and Vietnam was wrong, all wrong." LT felt a familiar rage rising within. Tamping it down he remembered something another retired Lieutenant Colonel told him while they were fishing along the Kenai Penninsula, "Ain't none of us always right, boy. It's how we behave after we find out we were wrong that matters."

Like now.

"I'm sorry too Dad," LT replied, feeling closer to his father than he had in too many long years.

"Sorry sons of bitches, that's what we are," the Lieutenant Colonel chuckled, then coughed, then fell back on the pillow. "Why don't you ask your mother to come in,son. She'll want to see we're not rolling around on the floor biting each other."

So LT did and for the first time in many long years the Baker family was once again acting like a family.

"The United States Border Patrol has invested a lot of money into training you Agent Ferrier. Your resignation is making that a very poor investment." Senior Agent Barnes was not happy with my resignation. Barnes was a good man, a good supervisor who more than once had cut me considerable slack as a probationary patrolman. Now I was leaving. He was disappointed. I was determined.

"I don't feel like I have the dedication, sir," I answered. "Not the kind you need to do this job properly. It's like that story about the little boy that puts his finger in the dike to stop the water from leaking out. Plug up one hole, five more appear. That's us, plugging up one hole while five more appear."

"That's what I hate about hiring college boys to do this job," Barnes barked. "They're all full of bullshit stories to justify their actions."

I couldn't tell whether he was serious or joking with me. I decided he was serious.

"You know sir, one night in Brownsville I was doing a four to midnight. When I came on shift we drove down to the dam across the Rio Grande and parked. My partner and I watched two wetbacks trying to climb the eight foot fence on the dam. There was a fat one and a skinny one. The skinny one scaled the fence and waited for his buddy. His buddy was too fat and couldn't get over. The skinny one tried to pull up the bottom of the fence so his friend could crawl under. He tugged and he strained to hold the fence up while the fat guy tried to wiggle under. When the fat guy was about halfway through his buddy loses his grip and the fence snaps down pinning the fat guy to the ground. The fat guy starts howling, his buddy can't budge the fence and my partner and I are laughing so hard we couldn't bring ourselves to go help. But we finally did. All three of us lifted the bottom of the fence high enough for the fat one to squirm through. He gets up, rubbing his belly where the fence had pinned him, says "Gracias Amigos" and starts to walk into Brownsville. The skinny one looks at us and starts to follow. They both looked surprised and disappointed when we hooked them up and brought them into the station."

"And your point is?" Senior Agent Barnes had heard tales like this his whole working life.

"Four hours later we're having coffee a little further down the river and the fat guy and the skinny guy come walking by us, grinning like idiots. They didn't see our prowler, or us until we hooked them up again, drove them to the station and put them in the cage. We didn't even bother with the paperwork because the van arrived and took everyone in the cage out to be Voluntarily Returned (VR'd)."*

"Your point is not emerging."

"So midnight and we're coming off shift. When we get to the station I go by the cage and there they are, fat and skinny, grinning away. I check the sheet and see they were picked up an hour before, back at the dam. Three times in one night. I started to question what we were doing after that."

"What we were doing, what we are doing, is our job. Our job is apprehending and detaining illegal immigrants who are crossing into the United States," Senior Agent Barnes pronounced, with appropriate authority.

"The system sucks, sir," I answered. "With all respect, good men on a fool's errand."

Special Agent Barnes didn't answer at first. He shuffled my resignation papers, then signed and endorsed them. Handing them back to me he said, "If that is the way you feel you should resign. Good luck ex-Agent Ferrier."

And the wheel turned again. Onward.

> *VR'd" is Immigration lingo for "Voluntarily
> Returned." If you can imagine being handcuffed,
> caged, put in a van, driven to a border crossing,
> un-handcuffed and being told to walk back into
> Mexico as "Voluntarily Returned."

Postscript

I spent just over a year in the United States Border Patrol.
During that time I had first hand, up front knowledge of how
difficult, demanding and impossible the job of patrolling our
southern border was then and is now.

Author with Rattle Snake, Border Control

Eight months on the Rio Grande river was enough for me to
fully appreciate why, in 476 BCE, the Chinese, then the most
advanced and cultured nation on the planet, began building
a 13,171 mile long, twenty five and half foot high wall

around their entire country. The fact that it ultimately didn't work for them either is not the point. The point is the Border Patrol taught me to understand why they built it.

What follows are two Border Patrol "war stories." They each happened to me in the relatively short time I was on the job. I cannot imagine the backlog of tales I could tell if I had stayed on the job any longer.

Romantic Ramon & The Bruja

About halfway through the sixteen week course of study at the Border Patrol Academy. I was on a four to midnight training shift outside Brownsville, Texas. Trainees such as I did a ride along with an experienced Patrolman to get the feel of the job. Because I was a veteran I got a lot more cache than the average trainee, two tours in Vietnam earned me that. Anyway after a rather routine tour of duty along the Brownsvillle-Matamoros border we were heading back to the station at around 11:45 PM. Cruising the fenceline on a two lane dirt track with a drainage ditch on one side and Mexico on the other. We were tired, hungry and ready to call it a night. Then we saw the pickup truck nose down in the drainage ditch, lights on, motor running nobody around.

"Think we oughta' check it out?" Walt Greening, my training officer asked as he slowed our prowler down.

I answered the mandatory yes and we parked just behind the vehicle, our headlights illuminating the truck. There looked to be no one in the cab and no one on the ground.

"Suppose you do a vehicle check," Walt more than suggested.

I got out of the prowler, drew my pistol and cautiously approached the ditched truck. Following all the Academy tactical instruction I peeped the passenger side window and saw a passed out and prone figure slumped across the front seat, head down in the passenger side foot well. The window was up. The guy looked like he was breathing. I tapped my flashlight on the window, no response. Walt had taken his position beside the driver side door of the prowler with a Remington Pump shotgun at the ready. I signalled to him one guy, not responsive. Walt motioned me to the driver side of the truck. The driver window was down and I could see the trucks interior plainly. Several Lone Star beer cans littered the front seat. The driver was face down on the floor, snoring. The cab smelled like a bad bar room. I reached through the window and turned off the ignition. No reaction from the driver.

"Sir, can you hear me? Are you injured?" I asked.

No reaction from the driver, just more snoring. Walt moved up to the passenger side of the vehicle, shotgun ready. Being careful not to cross Walt's line of fire I opened the driver side door. Still no reaction from the driver.

Walt motioned with his shotgun to the gun rack on the rear cab window. It held a Winchester repeater. I removed the rifle, placing it carefully in the bed of the truck. I poked the driver with my flashlight, keeping my pistol trained on him. The driver grunted and started trying to crawl out of the passenger hole.

"Slowly sir," I commanded, "you may be injured."

More grunting and squirming from the driver who finally managed to sit up, sort of, and wonder where he was. He did not appear injured. No blood, no bruises, no clue. He smelled of beer, lots of beer and piss. It looked like he had wet himself while keeled over, adding not one bit to his charm or character. I didn't see another weapon, gun or knife. I holstered my pistol and tried to help him sit up.

"Are you okay sir? Can you hear me?" I repeated.

He turned his head slowly, blearily to look at me. After due consideration he asked, "Who the fuck are you?"

Charming.

"United States Border Patrol," I answered, "we're going to get you some help."

"I don't need no help. What the fuck did you do to my truck?"

Oh boy. Walt was grinning, but he kept the shotgun on him.

"Let me help you out of there sir. We'll see if you're alright." I grabbed the wet and stinky driver by as little of his clothing as I could and started to slide him out of the truck. The closer he got the worse he smelled and the angrier he was becoming.

"Take your fucking hands off me," he growled, trying to stand up beside the truck.

I stepped back to get a better look at him. Little guy, maybe five-four, five-six, crew cut, beady eyes, buck teeth, muscular build, drunk as a monkey. He was wearing a red checkered cowboy shirt, soggy jeans, brown boots and an ill-omened snarl.

"You gonna' arrest me?" He grumbled.

Walt had walked around the back of the truck, removed the Winchester from the bed and stood, grinning. This was going to be my show. Training day.

"Are you a United States Citizen?" I asked, hoping to lighten the snarl.

"Fucking-A, I am. What's it to ya?" The snarl was back.

"We're the Border Patrol, you're a citizen, we're not going to arrest you," I tried. I also noticed Walt had gone back to the prowler and was on the radio, calling the Texas Highway Patrol no doubt, and they were definitely going to arrest him.

My Border Patrol answer silenced the driver for a moment. I noticed his hands were balled up into fists and that he was shuffling from foot to foot unsteadily. I was quiet, watching. The driver wasn't.

"I been arrested before you know," He announced.

"I don't care, sir. We're just going to get you a tow truck, get your vehicle out of the ditch."

He thought about that for a moment, grumbling to himself.

"Wanna' know what I was arrested for?" He half-shouted, getting belligerent while I was getting ready.

"No sir, I do not. Just stand there, be quiet and we'll get your truck out of the ditch in no time."

Which only seemed to make him madder. I took a step forward to try to calm him down. That's when he jumped me. When I say he jumped me, I mean he literally jumped me, like a big, wet, drunk frog. He shouted something as he leaped. It sounded like, "I fucked a cow!"

Before I knew it, he had wrapped his legs around my waist, his arms around my head and he was trying to chew through my brand-new Border Patrol hat. I staggered backwards, kept my balance and started trying to peel him off me. If I could have taken a moment to see what Walt was doing, I would have seen that he was laughing his ass off. And that's when the Texas Highway Patrol pulled up. There were two of them in the cruiser. They knew Walt. All three of them were now laughing their asses off.

When I finally managed to peel this asshole of me, I slammed him down on the ground, knelt on his back, handcuffed him and dragged him to his feet. Walt and the two Highway Patrolmen applauded.

"I see you've met Romantic Ramon," One of the Patrolman said.

"Who?" was all I could huff and puff as I slammed the drunken cowboy into the side of his truck.

"Romantic Ramon," the Patrolman repeated, "We picked him up a few months back for fucking a cow."

I silently prayed I wasn't hearing him correctly. I was wet as a sponge, beer, urine, spit and drool and my brand new Border patrol hat was a mess. I looked at Ramon in disbelief. He was snoring again, standing up.

Eventually I traded my cuffs back from the THP (Texas Highway Patrol), turned Ramon over to the officers, and Walt and I drove in for end of shift. Walt made me keep my window down all the way back, I had Ramon stink all over me. I spent the next hour at the station trying to write an incident report that sounded less ridiculous than what happened. By noon the next day the entire Staff and class of the Academy knew all about Ramon and my report didn't sound any less ridiculous than what happened.

The Bruja

It's a midnight to eight AM shift at the Sierra Blanca traffic checkpoint on Interstate 10 in Texas. I've been out of the Academy three months, successfully serving a probationary period required of all Academy graduates. I did well at the Academy and got along well at the Sierra Blanca station.

The checkpoint was manned sporadically. There were not enough Patrolmen in Sierra Blanca to keep it open full time, so we did the random spot check of traffic coming off the freeway, routing the vehicles through a roadside rest area where we gave them a quick once over and waved them on. Most of the time.

There were a lot of tourist vehicles on the late shift, out of state plates, vaguely lost looking drivers with a car full of sleeping passengers, tractor trailers taking advantage of the open roads and cooler temperatures and a certain amount of transients and nocturnal people travelling late at night to attract as little attention to themselves as possible.

There were always three of us at the checkpoint. Two on the ground waving at cars and one roaming around in the chase car in case someone got antsy and made a run for it. I loved the chase car. Tonight, I was on the ground waving at cars. The hard part was staying awake, staying alert.

Suddenly, on the ramp leading into the checkpoint a car stopped, hesitated, started to turn around, couldn't, and reluctantly started creeping forward. The vehicle was a classic border junker, one headlight, no front bumper, lots of exhaust smoke and a rusting, faded paint job. I had no idea how the driver could possibly see through the amount of dirt on the windshield and doubted the car was going to make it to the stop sign, but it did, and that's when the fun started.

The driver was a heavy set Hispanic woman who looked to be in her fifties. She had a colorful scarf tied around her head, gypsy style, a lot of clinking jewelry and four male passengers who looked like they were on their way to the illegal alien hall of fame.

"Good evening Ma'am. Where are you headed this evening?" I asked as she cranked down the filthy driver side window.

'Van Horn," she answered in heavily accented English. Van Horn was a community about thirty miles east.

"Are you a citizen of the United States?" I continued.

"I was born in Van Horn," She answered.

"Are your passengers all going to Van Horn as well?"

She didn't answer, looking straight ahead. I tried again. "Are your passengers going to Van Horn?" Nothing.

Okay, enough. "Ma'am would you pull you car over to the left and shut off your engine please." Without saying a word she creaked the car over to the holding area. I turned to the trailer and asked Jesse, my back up, to man the checkpoint while I go talk to this crew.

This time I tried the passengers. "Buenas noches, amigos. Donde va, esta noche?"

No answer. Nobody looked at me. Two of them giggled. I had enough.

"Todos fuera del coche!" I barked, ordering everybody out of the car. Nobody moved. The gigglers giggled. I turned my attention back to the driver.

"Ma'am I need you to get out of the car. Right now." She started to wiggle her way out from under the steering wheel while I shouted over to Jesse. "Jess, call in the prowler and ask him to come over here."

Jess waved okay and made the radio call for the prowler. Jesus Barnes was in the prowler and never very far away. Jesus had been raised along the border and his Spanish and knowledge of the native folk was much better than mine. I left the four grinning amigos in the car and started to question the driver.

She told me her name was Maria Gonzales-Gonzalez and she produced a valid Texas driver's license with a Van Horn address. When I asked again about her passengers she cast a worried look back at her car and finally said she had picked them up hitchhiking a few miles back and knew nothing about them.

The thing about "a few miles back" was that there was nothing but open desert back there all the way to El Paso. Nobody, but nobody picks up four male hitchhikers in the middle of the night in the middle of nowhere. Just then Jesus pulled up.

I brought him up to speed and he walked over to the car and jerked the front seat passenger out by the scruff of his neck. The back seat amigos looked horrified, then began arguing among themselves. I couldn't understand what they were arguing about but Maria suddenly looked worried as Jesus tip-toed the front seat passenger over to the prowler and began questioning him.

Nobody here looked or acted dangerous but the argument in the back seat of Maria's car was getting louder so I went over and told them to quiet down. This only made them argue more. Jesus stashed the front seat passenger in the back of the prowler and walked over to where I had Maria and began to ask her questions in rapid fire, largely unintelligible (by me) Spanish.

When he was satisfied he pulled me aside with a huge grin on his face.

"You're not going to believe this one," He said. That was not hard for me to accept.

"These boys believe Maria is a bruja, a witch. They paid her to drive them to Van Horn where they hoped to find jobs. She sprinkled them with turkey bone powder which she claimed would make them invisible, they would only be seen if one of them stopped believing he was invisible. They are arguing about which of them stopped believing."

"Maria is going with a just picked them up hitchhiking story," I answered.

"Yeah, that figures. Look, I'll run them all into the station, hold them till morning and ship them into El Paso. Let them figure this out. You however get to write this one up, that way if El Jefe in El Paso is looking for a new witch catcher you get to be it."

Which is what happened, only I never caught another witch.

Chapter Five

Confessions

The logistics were a nightmare, Christmas holiday travelers filled the airports, filled the airplanes. I flew from El Paso, Texas to New York, then spent four hours in a plastic chair waiting for my flight to Orly Airport in Paris. Next was an eight-hour flight across the Atlantic, trying to sleep sitting up, not succeeding. When we deplaned, Orly Airport looked like any other terminal I had ever been in except the signs were all in French. I followed the herd to customs. A brief look at me, a stamp on my passport and there she was, standing by the barrier outside customs arrivals.

The first thing I noticed was the smile. Her smile. The one I had known since third grade, the one that lit up my heart and soul. The second thing I noticed was the rakish green beret, the Christmassy red scarf, and again, the smile, then the pounding in my chest as I hurried to her.

"You're here!" Margaret Mary exclaimed as she leaped into my arms. I spun her around, two full turns, before I could let her go and say, "I am, and you look wonderful!" Which resulted in two more spins.

"Your luggage," she said, "and then we go home!"

"Where's Josephine?" I teased.

"You must not call her that! If you do, I will kick you and then Gianna will kick you as well."

I agreed and then there was luggage, a bus, a very clean, brightly lit subway, long flights of upward bound stairs and Paris! I had no idea where I was in the city, but the streets were cobblestones, the houses neatly aligned in red brick and the streetlights were gas lit and charming. Christmas wreaths and Christmas holly were everywhere, twinkling lights reflected in a light dusting of snow made the moonlight magical. So far this was so much better than so good.

Margaret Mary had not let go of my arm throughout the entire trip from the airport, asking me a thousand questions I don't remember my answers to. I was exhilarated, exhausted, enchanted and in Paris. It didn't look anything like Texas.

"Thirty days suspension. No pay. I suggest you use this time constructively Officer Gianoulis. Your next offense will not end in a suspension. You will be fired."

Teddy could not meet his supervisor's eyes as he heard his sentence. The suspension was not for Drunk on Duty, which he was, but for excessive force, which he used in subduing a juvenile who did not want to get in the patrol car after being arrested. Teddy was doing a lot of that lately. He had become known as a street bully, a bad cop. His supervisors were aware of his reputation and growing very short of patience with his performance.

"Buncha shit," Teddy growled as he emptied his locker. His partner, Mike Stanns, didn't think so, but couldn't say so.

"A month's not so bad, Ted. You'll get it back," Mike offered.

"Not if I find another job first," Teddy said as he stormed out of the station house. Mike could hardly disguise his relief.

Merry Christmas, Lowell. A bad cop was off the streets.

Beth had not returned to their apartment in three months. Teddy had not seen his daughter, Samanatha, in that time and didn't try to. His sister, Connie, was no longer speaking to him. Kevin had asked him not to come around the gym. His father was living with his sister in Greece and would have been ashamed of him if he was here. And Teddy blamed all this on everybody but himself.

"Fuck off Peter. I told you I didn't want any part of this lawsuit bullshit." Teddy slammed the phone down on Peter Rayburn after doing the same thing when Cindy had called him earlier. The Agent Orange class action case was moving forward. Teddy was an original claimant, his daughter, Samantha, a grievous example of the consequences of the spraying and yet Teddy was withdrawing, not just from the lawsuit, but from everybody and everything.

"I'm going up there," Peter announced, "I've known Teddy since we were kids. Maybe I can talk some sense into him."

Cindy hoped so, Horatio hoped so. Since Peter and Cindy had joined Horatio's law firm in Baltimore, they had signed up over six hundred veterans to the Agent Orange lawsuit taking place across the country. Thousands of veterans had come forward with tragic personal stories of cancers, malignancies, rashes, liver diseases and the most tragic of all - birth defects among their children. All could document extensive exposure to herbicides during their tour in Vietnam. A horrible picture of purposeful neglect was taking shape. Someone, somebody had to be held accountable. Peter, Cindy and former Captain Horatio Marks, among a nationwide network of Vietnam veteran activists, were going to see to it.

Peter took a train, a bus and a taxicab to arrive at Teddy and Beth's apartment the next day. He found Teddy, no Beth, no Samantha, and the wreckage of a man who used to be his friend. Teddy had gained thirty pounds, his face was bloated, his eyes bloodshot, his appearance slovenly and drunken. He would not let Peter into the apartment.

"I told you to leave me alone, Peter. I meant it. Screw." Teddy started to slam the apartment door. Peter put out his hand and stopped him. Anger flashed through Teddy's eyes.

"Ted, please, just give me a minute. We need you; your daughter needs you. Please."

Teddy hesitated, then stepped aside and lumbered back into the apartment. Peter followed. The place was a mess. It smelled of old beer cans, dirty laundry and despair. Teddy flopped onto a sofa. Peter cleared debris from a chair and sat down. He opened his briefcase and took out a sheaf of documents which he offered to Teddy. Teddy showed no interest in them.

"We have over a thousand vets now, Ted. All across the country. All of them are making statements, showing medical records, offering testimony about Agent Orange exposure. We need you, Ted. This one," Peter held out a page, "documents the time you spent in I Corps during your tour. This one," Peter shuffled pages, "is a terrain map showing the areas in I Corps which were intensively defoliated using these herbicides. These are Samantha's medical records; we have forty similar cases among the vets who have come forward. We are taking this to trial, Ted."

Ted looked up, bleary eyed and hurt. "What do we get if we win, Peter, Does Samantha get a new spine?"

Peter dropped the paperwork at Ted's feet. "Samantha gets the medical treatment she needs to live the best life she can, Ted. I'm not a doctor. I don't know what can be done and what can't for your daughter. But as a lawyer I can make sure she gets everything she needs and deserves. Help us help her."

"It's all my fault you know," Teddy groaned, "I volunteered to go there, I volunteered to stay there. I thought I was doing the right thing, instead I ruined my baby."

"The government ruined your baby, Ted. The generals, the politicians, whoever the hell authorized the use of this poison. They should be held accountable for what they did, not you holding yourself accountable for what happened to Samantha."

"Nothing would have happened to Samantha if it hadn't been for me!" Teddy bellowed.

"Perhaps nothing would have happened to Samantha if the government had not sprayed you and thousands of other soldiers with a deadly defoliant, they knew to be toxic and harmful to humans."

Teddy considered the papers scattered at his feet. "What do you want me to do?"

"I need you to sign the declaration. And I may need you to testify in the future."

"Testify to what?" Teddy sounded suspicious, angry, reluctant.

"The truth, Ted, just the truth. This isn't about me talking you into doing something. This is about you doing the right thing."

Teddy signed. Peter left. The apartment still smelled of old beer cans, dirty laundry and despair.

This was going to be Lieutenant Colonel Robert Baker's last Christmas. He had stopped his chemotherapy three times a week four days ago and was resting, and dying, in the master bedroom of his home in Philadelphia. LT and his mother were at his bedside. A hospice nurse eased his pain. He slept most of the time. LT and his mother watched and waited.

"Water please," the colonel croaked, gratefully accepting the glass LT offered. Sipping carefully, he smiled and reached for his wife's hand. Fighting back her tears Lois Baker squeezed her husband's hand gently. The colonel whispered, "It's close now. I can feel it, like sleep coming on."

LT was finding it hard to breathe, tears ran freely down his mother's face. The colonel smiled again, "Please don't be sad. Only my body is dying, the rest of me is going to be right here with you."

LT had never heard his father philosophize so, speaking gently and with compassion for them, never pity for himself. LT was as proud as he was sad as he watched his father's life fading away.

"Come close son," the colonel whispered again. LT moved closer to the bedside, bent down to hear his father's faint voice, "Take care of your mother, she's a better woman than I have ever been a husband." LT could only nod in response, his voice choked silent by sadness. "Take care of yourself as well. I'm proud of you, I should have been prouder."

Then, with a sigh, Lieutenant Colonel Robert Baker died. It was Christmas Eve, 1975. The world had lost a good man. A generation of good men were passing. These soldiers who defeated Hitler and Imperial Japan, that held the line in Korea and wept over the debacle of Vietnam. Time and life and nature were taking them away, unnoticed, unrecognized, un-mourned, except for their families.

LT and his mother stepped aside as the hospice nurse bent over the colonel. She looked up at them, shook her head and composed the body as best she could. Silence filled the Silent Night.

"Who's on the mat now Ted?" Kevin demanded when he stopped by Teddy's apartment on his way home from the gym. "A while ago you were telling me I had my eight count and it was time to get up, remember?"

Somewhere, down beneath the puddle of vodka and beer Teddy felt shame as he listened to Kevin. He clenched his fists and listened, unable to meet Kevin's eyes.

"Ma asked me to come by and invite you to Christmas dinner tomorrow. Beth and your daughter would like to see you too, if you're sober."

"I gotta' gift for Samantha," Teddy muttered, "Beth too."

"The gift they need is you Ted, why don't you get off your ass and give yourself to them? You think I don't know something about being ashamed of myself for something that turns out to be not your fault? I know how much it hurts and how hard it is to let go of the guilt. You helped me with mine, Ted. Let us help you with yours."

Teddy didn't answer, couldn't answer. He was too deep into his pain, too comfortable in his misery. "I'll come by in the morning."

"Do that," Kevin replied, "then you can spend the rest of the day feeling sorry for yourself." Kevin turned to the door, "And take a shower, you smell like piss and Budweiser. Merry Christmas."

"So, what is this special announcement, this big question you have got me all the way over here to ask me?" I asked as we sat sipping really good wine in Margaret Mary and Gianna's living room on Christmas Eve.

My first meeting with Margaret Mary's girlfriend (there, I said it), was delightful, dammit. Gianna turned out to be witty, wonderful and wise. She greeted me with a warm embrace, smiled with her eyes and welcomed me to their home. She had a million questions about Texas, cowboys and the Wild, Wild West. I hammed it up of course, modestly relating my epic adventures in the sagebrush. Once or twice, I noticed Margaret Mary's tolerant smile at my tales, but she didn't give me away, she is my buddy.

Their affection for one another was plain and simple and true. Of course I was jealous of Gianna, but me being me, I knew I could never be for Margaret Mary what Gianna was, a partner, a lover, a companion and a soul mate. I still had that apart thing going on, always had, always will.

In the three days since I arrived in Paris I had been on a whirlwind tour, a carousel of sights and sounds and tastes and wonders of the most beautiful city I had ever seen. I had been to the Eiffel Tower (of course), the Louvre, strolled the Champs-Elysees, ogled the Rose Windows of Notre Dame Cathedral, visited the Musee d'Orsay, the wonderful, old, converted train station housing works of art by Monet, Van

Gogh, Degas and Renoir and many others, all of whom Margaret Mary was able to identify and rhapsodize about.

We had taken the 45-minute train ride to the palace of Versailles, eaten numerous exotic meals consisting of dishes whose names I could not pronounce and delighted in the view of Paris from the courtyard of the Sacre Coeur church which was within walking distance of La Premiere Impression II, Margaret Mary and Gianna's brilliant gallery of art.

One afternoon as we sipped espresso in a West Bank café, while I listened to Margaret Mary convey her love for this city, I realized I had never felt this way about anywhere. I really hoped someday I would. Perhaps this was the place for me. I had no real ties elsewhere, maybe I could move here, stay here, find a life here.

Man plans, God laughs. And it was going to get worse.

My question about Margaret Mary's question still hung in the Christmas Eve evening as more wine was passed around and a warm glow descended on the apartment.

"Our question is not for tonight," Margaret Mary answered, "it is our Christmas wish, and we shall wish it tomorrow."

Gianna nodded in agreement, and I had just enough wine in me to let the matter lie. The apartment was warm and glowing with a fire in the fireplace, a perfect Christmas tree smothered in gaily wrapped presents twinkled in the corner of the room, soft carols echoed from outside the windows and a light snow was falling. What could go wrong?

"Tell us more about Texas," Gianna pleaded, more than half in the bag, as we all were getting. "Did you ever meet John Wayne?"

Margaret Mary snarfed into her wine glass as I considered spinning a wild and completely fabricated tale about me and the Duke. Then the phone rang. Overseas operator, Margaret Mary reported, from Dublin.

"Nullaig Shona Duit!" Margaret Mary repeated into the telephone after hearing the traditional Gaelic Christmas greeting from far away Dublin.

"Oh Da, it's wonderful! David is here, our Yule log is burning, it snowed today, only yourself and Rose are missing."

"As it is here without your presence, dear Daughter." Sean replied. "Your aunt is right here, and we miss you terribly."

News was exchanged, promises were made, the phone was passed all around and a yearning tear or two flowed before they rang off. Stillness descended in the apartment once again as I forgot the details of my imaginary meeting with the Duke.

"David, did you have romances while you were in Texas?" Gianna asked, forgetting about the Duke.

"A cowboy only loves his horse," I answered, hoping that didn't sound too bestial.

Gianna looked puzzled. Margaret Mary looked curious. "I must admit," I continued, "I did like cowgirls better than cowboys or my horse, but no romance. My heart is for now, silent." And I snuck a look at Margaret Mary who did not meet my eye.

The rest of the evening was semi-quiet, pleasant, two bottles of Bordeaux-ish before we tottered off to our respective beds, mine alone, where I waited for morning to hear Margaret Mary's Christmas wish.

As I lay in my solitary Parisian guest room bed a song drifted into my head. Non-Christmassy as it was, it somehow echoed my feelings of hope, happiness and uncertain melancholy. I heard the trio of Crosby, Stills and Nash sing...

Helplessly hoping a harlequin hovers nearby,
Awaiting a word,
Gasping at glimpses of gentle true spirit he
runs,
Wishing he could fly,
Only to trip at the sound of goodbye.

Wordlessly watching he waits by the window
and wonders,
At the empty space inside.

Heartlessly helping himself to her bad dreams,
he worries,
Did he hear a goodbye?
Or a hello?

They are one person,
They are two alone,
They are three together,
They are four for each other.

Stand in the stairway,
You'll see something certain to tell you,
Confusion has its cost.
Love isn't lying,
It's loose in a lady who lingers,
Saying she is lost, and choking, on hello.

They are one person,
They are two alone,
They are three together,
They are four for each other. *

As I hoped we all could be for each other in the New Year to come.

Lyrical Aspirations:
Helplessly Hoping, Stephen Stills

Chapter Six

Yuletide

Christmas morning in Paris was magical. I awoke to the smell of fresh coffee, French Roast of course, baking croissants, and pine scented incense burning from the living room. Gianna was doing kitchen duty; Margaret Mary was fussing about with plates and cups and knives and forks. I gathered up the hidden treasures I had brought with me from Texas and entered the living room full of smiles. Let the gifting begin.

"First we eat, then we share gifts, then we talk, the question, no?" Gianna announced cryptically as she delivered a tray holding coffee, croissants and jam.

The question, yes. I was sure I knew what they were going to ask and couldn't wait to say yes. Man plans, God laughs, yet again.

The coffee was strong, the croissants warm and toasty, the jam was sweet. As we put aside our "petit dejeuner," breakfast, to the common folk, Margaret Mary handed me an elegantly wrapped gift that looked almost too pretty to tear apart. Almost.

Wrapped in my brand new, Euro-correct, "echarpe," which should mean "sexy guy scarf," I handed Margaret Mary and Gianna each a turquoise and silver necklace and bracelet set straight out of El Paso, Texas. Cowgirls indeed. Oohs and ah's followed, more trinkets were exchanged, more laughter and love shared and then, THE QUESTION.

Margaret Mary and Gianna sat very close together on the sofa. I was cross-legged on the floor. You could cut the anticipation with a knife. I knew, you see, what these two were up to. Obviously, they had found some exotic locale where two people of the same persuasion could be married. I had seen for almost a week how perfect these two were together. I was going to be part of the ceremony. I was happy for them. Dammit.

They joined hands. Margaret Mary spoke first. Was she blushing? Looking me dead in the eye, she began, "David, I want you to make a baby with me."

"And with me as well," Gianna added.

I was speechless. I blinked a lot. My mouth moved, no sounds came out, no words came to mind. I was trying to process the enormity of what they were asking. I was recognizing what an immeasurable compliment I was being paid. And I was speechless.

"Oh David, we will raise our babies here, as brother and sister or brother and brother or sister and sister," Margaret

Mary continued, breathless and all in a rush as she was when she was excited. And she was blushing.

"Our children will be "enfants magnifique" and you shall be their father and come to visit us whenever you can and be with your babies as well," Gianna added. She was not blushing.

Dumbfounded as I was, I knew my response was going to be very, very disappointing. Without a word I got up and sat between Margaret Mary and Gianna on the sofa. I took each of their hands in mine and started the most uncomfortable and sad confession of my life. "I have to tell you something I have never told anyone," I began, unable to look at them, "My parents don't know this, nobody knows this. You are the first."

This story was not going to get any easier to tell if I related the long version, so I jumped right in. "Last year, after Teddy's baby was born, when I learned she may never walk, or even sit up straight, I went and had some blood tests done."

Margaret Mary immediately made the connection. Gianna looked confused. I continued, explaining mainly to her, "Our friend Teddy and his wife Beth's baby was born with spinal bifida occulta and a cleft palate. The doctor's say this most likely resulted from Ted's exposure to Agent Orange, a defoliant used to kill the jungle in Vietnam. I was in the same parts of Vietnam Teddy was and I was there twice as long."

"This Agent Orange was a bad thing?" Gianna asked as Margaret Mary fought with her tears.

"They sprayed it from airplanes all around us, all over us. They told us it was harmless to humans. Now thousands of

Vietnam veterans and uncounted Vietnamese civilians are having children with horrible birth defects."

Silence smothered the room. It didn't feel like Christmas anymore. Margaret Mary was openly sobbing. Gianna was silent. I staggered on, "I couldn't face the possibility that any child I fathered would be born that way. A couple of weeks after Samantha was born, I went to a doctor and had a vasectomy. I cannot, will not, have children."

Margaret Mary put her arms around me as she cried. Up to that moment I had never questioned, never regretted my decision. Now I felt a great emptiness, a great void in my heart. My eyes filled with tears, that all too familiar lump choked my throat, and I tried to squeak out an apology, but to who? And for what?

We sat and held each other in the Christmas morning silence. Gianna recovered first. She rose and gathered coffee cups and plates and without a word took them to the kitchen. Christmas was lost, sorrow filled the room.

"Oh David, I'm so sorry," Margaret Mary whispered when we were alone.

I was sorry as well. I was sorry for Margaret Mary and Gianna. I was sorry for me. I was sorry for how much that war had changed and hurt me and was hurting people I loved. I feared how much it would continue to do so in the future.

"Merry Christmas, Ma!" Eddie intoned, handing his mother a red, white and blue envelope. "They're Sox tickets, Ma. For you and Camille. I got Opening Day, Sox Yankees, then the Orioles, Indians and Twins."

Eddie's mother, Hazel, smiled and handed the tickets to her sister. More smiles, then another gift. "We're movin' Ma. I found us a place over on Harrison, right near the Holy Cross Cathedral. First floor, Ma, no more stairs."

Eddie's mother was dumbfounded, as was her sister, Camille. They had lived in their third floor walk up apartment for thirty years, ever since Eddie was born. She knew the streets, the stores, her neighbors, everything about the neighborhood. Still, the stairs were becoming a challenge, the streets more crowded, the neighbors moving away.

"Harrison is it? We can't afford to live there! Rich and snooty they are!" Hazel replied.

"We can afford it, Ma. I'm getting' a second cab. Mickey Ginty's gonna' drive for me. We've got the dough."

"Harrison Street and a second cab on what you make driving a hack?" Camille said, hardly concealing her skepticism.

"I'm doin' real good, Cam, lotsa' airport runs, businessman types. They tip good," Eddie offered.

"You are also laying off bets with Paddy the Barber and Charlie Shay down at Milligan's Pub," Hazel added.

Eddie was embarrassed. He tried to keep his extra-curriculars low key around the house.

"It's just a few bucks, Ma, couple hundred, honest."

"Charley Shay tells me you're doin' a bit more than that on just the Celtics and the Bruins," Camille said.

"You know what that nice lawyer lady told you Eddie, you get caught again, you're goin' inside, nothin' they can do will save ya'," Hazel added.

"I'm not gonna' get caught, Ma. I'm keepin' it small. Locals only, meat and potatoes bets, no fancy stuff. Nobody gets in trouble for that."

So said The Fool.

Teddy was on his best behavior, sober as he ever got to be, which is to say hung over and miserable. He was seated in the living room of Beth's mother house with his wife and daughter. Kevin and his mother hovered nearby, in the kitchen. The living room had a tinseled Christmas tree, several brightly wrapped, unopened gifts and an orthopedic chair which allowed Samantha to sit upright, as smiling and happy as Teddy and Beth were grim and silent.

"How long are you on suspension for?" Beth finally asked.

"'Nother week," Teddy replied.

"Does your insurance still cover you? Samantha has to go to the doctors."

"I still got insurance, no pay though," Teddy growled, "Buncha' shit."

"It's not a bunch of shit, Teddy. You broke that kid's arm," Beth replied.

"He's lucky I didn't break his head. I tell him to get in the car, he better get his ass in the car."

What's happening to you, Ted? You didn't used to be this way," Beth said.

"Nuthin' happened to me," Teddy replied, then snuck a look at his daughter. Beth noticed.

"Sam is going to be fitted for a back brace next week," Beth offered, "then she can start some physical therapy so she can walk."

"Is that supposed to make me feel good?" Teddy replied bitterly, and loudly.

"Yes! It is!" Beth demanded, rising from the sofa and standing in front of Teddy. Kevin tensed in the kitchen doorway. "Your daughter is receiving the best treatment we can get her, or I can get her, I should say. She's happy and smiling and wonderful and look at you! You can't even shave or clean up to come over on Christmas? You smell like..."

"Budweiser and piss," Kevin added, coming into the room. "Maybe it's time you should go, Ted."

"You gonna' make me?" Teddy demanded.

"If I have to," Kevin replied as Beth's mother, Gloria came into the room as a peacemaker.

"I'll not have this in my house! Not on Christmas, not ever!" She shouted. Samantha began to cry. So did Beth. Teddy stormed out the door. Kevin slammed it shut.

Ho-ho-ho.

"You sure you're going to be alright, Mom?" LT asked on Christmas Day, the day after Lieutenant Colonel Robert Baker passed away. Mother and son were in the living room of the house. No Christmas decorations here, save an unopened card or two in red or green envelopes lying forgotten on a table.

"I'm going to sell the house and move to Fort Lauderdale with my sister. She lost your uncle John two years ago and has invited me to come stay with her."

"You're sure?"

"Staying here would be too full of memories. I think Florida will be best."

So, it was settled. LT's mother would pack up for Florida, LT would return to Alaska. Families don't split much further apart than that.

"Are you happy up there Bobby?" His mom asked, calling him as always by his childhood name.

"I'm responsible for over 150 miles of coastline, Mom. I keep out poachers, unlicensed hunters, I protect endangered animals, I clear streams from flooding, I give aid and help to campers. Every day Mom I do something to make that part of the world a better place."

"That's wonderful Bobby. Will you come see me in Florida?"

"Only when it snows in Alaska Mom, and that's a lot."

Three days later Lieutenant Colonel Robert Baker was interred in the local Veteran's Cemetery next to a plot reserved for his wife and another, for his son, should he choose to be buried there. LT flew back to Alaska the following day.

Semper Fi.

"Being of the Jewish persuasion in no way exempts you from the traditional and expensive custom of bestowing gifts on your colleagues, employees and friends during this non-denominational holiday season," Peter chided.

"And since we are all three, copious amounts of gifts are called for," Cindy added.

Horatio was backed into a corner. His initial line of defense had crumbled. Fortunately, the corner he was backed into held two brand new, embossed leather briefcases, one for Peter, one for Cindy. In return Horatio was gratified to receive a Cross pen and pencil set he had once admired in their company, along with a Baltimore Orioles team baseball hat.

"On a more professional level," Horatio began, "we are going to bill into the Agent Orange lawsuit at $75 dollars an hour which we will split equally three ways. Of course, that means we won't get paid anything until there is a settlement. Meanwhile you two barristers are going to have to start earning your keep."

Peter looked at Cindy. Cindy looked at Horatio. Cindy began, "There is an opening in the Public Defender's office up in Lowell. Peter and I have applied. Naturally, they will hire Peter because he's a man. I could start a small private practice there and we could get by on Peter's salary while we work the Agent Orange case."

"They will hire Peter because he is THE man. 345, I recall, says it all."

"You are wearing that one out love," Cindy replied, charmingly.

"Lowell is your hometown, Peter?"

Peter nodded.

"Good veteran town too, isn't that where your buddy Dave is from?" Horatio asked.

"Yes, we can run an ad in the local paper, sign up some vets for the lawsuit."

"Good, it's settled then, you guys are off to Lowell, we work together on the Agent Orange case, and I write great things with my new pen and pencil set."

And they would.

In Paris, the joy had been pretty much sucked out of Christmas. Gloom replaced gaiety and though we tried we could not resurrrect the holiday spirit. Unborn babies filled our thoughts.

"This operation that you had, it is forever?" Gianna asked when we had a moment alone.

"The operation could be reversed, unfortunately Agent Orange is forever, I could never take the chance, Gianna."

"She is quite heartbroken you know," Gianna said indicating Margaret Mary who sat alone on their spacious veranda.

"I'm not doing so well myself," I admitted. "It means a lot to me that you two would even consider having me to be the father of your children."

Gianna hugged me then and kissed me on the cheek. "You should go to her, she is very sad."

Paris in December is a lot like Lowell in December, or Boston, or New York. It is cold, rainy or snowy and, though I never would have believed it three days ago, a bit melancholy. Which is how I found it when I joined Margaret Mary on the veranda.

"Im sorry," was all I could think of to say as I sat beside her. She put her head on my shoulder and whispered, "Me too."

So we sat and watched the snow turn to a slushy rain as the day wore on. Gianna announced that she was going to go by the gallery and see that all was well. When we were alone Mrgaret Mary asked, "What will you do now, David?"

As if I knew. Taking my best guess I answered, "Go back to Lowell I suppose, regroup."

"Lowell is not for you, David. Lowell is who you were, who we were. You should stay here. You could live with us until you find your own place."

I gulped at the very idea. Live in Paris? Me? A Lowell guy? It didn't seem likely.

"Truth is," I finally admitted, "I'm not brave enough. I don't know what I'd do here, just like I don't know what I'm going to do there. But if I was here every day would remind me that I disappointed you and soon I would begin to disappoint myself."

"I am disappointed, David, but it was not you who disappointed me. I understand why you did what you did. Maybe someday it will get better."

"Will the offer still be open?" I asked.

"If ever I have a child, you will be the father," She replied as my heart leaped, fell and broke. "You must remember, David, you are not just you, you are us. It doesn't matter if I am here and you are there or anywhere or anything, part of you will always be us as you will always be part of me."

I listened but did not hear until she whispered, "And I will always love you."

I could never figure how she could be so smart and I could be so dumb. That afternoon we walked to the art gallery and joined Gianna. We tried, hard, to take our minds off what had occured between us on Christmas mornng. And failed. Two gloomy days later I flew back to Boston. All the way across the Atlantic a sad, sad song, echoed through my head as I imagined Margaret Mary's face out the window of the airplane…

What'll I do
When you are far away
And I am blue
What'll I do?

What'll I do
When I am wondering who
Is kissing you
What'll I do?

What'll I do
With just a photograph
To tell my troubles to?

When I'm alone
With only dreams of you
That won't come true
*What'll I do?**

And the flight flew onward, or backward. Or forward. I was too sad to notice.

Lyrical Aspirations:
What'll I Do?   Irving Berlin

Chapter Seven

Homecomings

"Y"ou wouldn't have liked me, Dad. I was getting so I didn't like myself."

My Dad and I were talking on the ride back to Lowell from Logan airport in Boston. I was trying to explain my decision to leave the Border Patrol. My flight from Paris had been long, quite long enough for me to carefully consider my past and hazily contemplate my future. I was pushing thirty years old and hadn't found my footing yet. Not my vocational footing anyway. I had the Army behind me, and college and now the Border Patrol. Behind me was stacking up. I had to start dealing with what was in front of me.

"Sometimes finding out what's not right for you is just as important as discovering what is right for you," He answered as we sped north on Route 95. It was just the two of us, my Mom didn't feel good, he said, and my brothers were out about their own business. I was glad. I hadn't had a good talk with my Dad in way too long.

"When did you find out, Dad? What was right for you I mean."

"By the time I was your age son, you and your brothers were already born. Finding out what was right for me became less important than taking care of all of you."

I let that sink in. "What do you think you would have been, Dad, if it wasn't for us?"

Dad didn't answer right away. The car got quiet. Then with a grin he said, "Unhappy."

That's the kind of man my Dad was.

"I think we should get married."

"Why don't you get back to me when that's more than just a thought," Cindy answered while unpacking boxes in their new Lowell apartment. She did not stop unpacking and she did not look at Peter.

Peter stuttered and started over, "I mean we should get married."

Cindy stopped unpacking and gave Peter THE LOOK.

"We SHOULD each lose ten pounds and stop drinking so much Mateus Rose." She popped open another box of books and went back to work.

"You're making this very hard for me," Peter replied.

"Imagine what it would be like if we were married," Cindy warned. The box unpacking stopped. The waiting began.

Finally, Peter took a deep breath, got down on one knee and said, "I love you and I want you to be my wife. Will you marry me?"

"Of course I'll marry you. Why would you ever think I wouldn't?"

They set a date and kept unpacking.

Lawyers in love.

"Holt Creek is a mess and Bascomb Bay's getting' all the run-off from that loggin' company again. Ain't been nobody checkin' on 'em since you went away," Tom Carron complained at the Hume Town Hall meeting when LT returned from his father's funeral.

"Poachers been taking up traps over Bass Point," Micah Keys added.

"Zoomer Park's campground looks like a junk yard," Alice Minton said, waving her hand at the podium where LT stood.

The "Welcome Home" portion of the town meeting had ended and LT now faced the friendly, but cranky crowd of his neighbors and friends. Questions and problems came fast, but friendly, and when the meeting broke up LT and Alaska State Trooper Luke Drayber retired to the late Colonel Hackleberry's favorite table for coffee, without.

"Seems like the whole town's kinda' gone to blazes since you left," Luke chuckled as LT tried to figure out how to deal with the town's questions, complaints and comments. The fact was, in the year or so that LT had lived in Hume he had become a vital and valued member of the community. He was glad to be back, and anxious to resume the work they had entrusted him with.

"Few things there I'm going to need your help fixing," LT suggested.

"Nothing we can't work out," Luke answered. "You know, these folks have come to depend on you quite a bit."

"And me on them, Luke. I like it here, I belong here. All the time I was 'down below' I thought about how much nicer it is up here."

"Glad to hear that, LT, because there's one more thing I want to go over with you." Luke added. "Folks here have been talking about having their own lawman around here. Right now I'm all they've got and I have 165 miles of highway and the rest of the back country to take care of."

"You mean like a police force?" LT said.

"Not a police force, there's not enough funding for that. I'm talking about a constable."

"What the hell is a constable?" LT asked as he sipped his coffee, without.

"Constables's like a sheriff, a peace officer elected by the people by petition. He'd have the power of arrest, the authority to serve warrants, and be kind of a local judge on civil matters."

"Man like that isn't likely to remain popular very long," LT added.

"Depends on the man. A good man is likely to do a good job," Luke replied.

"Who do they have in mind?" LT asked.

"You." Luke grinned and sipped his coffee.

"Me?" LT was flabbergasted. "I already have a job. I like my job. I don't want to stop being a game warden."

"You wouldn't have to. I checked with Fairbanks. They said you could do both."

"I don't want to do both! Game warden keeps me pretty damn busy enough."

"Look, LT, the town can't afford a police force, or even a full time cop. The State can afford another game warden down here. You'd get an assistant, someone to help you out with the state stuff while you oversee any local issues."

LT chewed on that thought for a while. He realized it was an honor to have the townsfolk offer him the job. He loved the community and wanted to do all he could to make it a better, safer place. But a constable?

"This assistant, I'd still be in charge?" He asked.

"Senior Warden, the new man would work for you."

"And this constable would work with you as a backup?" LT was getting interested.

"I'd work with you as a friend, and as a fellow lawman," Luke replied.

"Would I get a badge?"

"I reckon we could dig one up for you someplace," Luke replied.

"I'm in," LT decided.

And the road rambled onward.

"So how was Paris? How is Margaret Mary?" My Dad asked as we rolled on toward home.

I wasn't quite sure how to begin telling that tale. I had never been really specific about Margaret Mary's relationship with Gianna, nor had I said anything about my decision not to risk fathering any children.

"Paris was great Dad. The finest place I've ever been. Margaret Mary and her girlfriend are running an art gallery which is very successful, and the city is beautiful."

"Girlfriend?" Dad said, eyes front and driving.

"Yeah," I hesitated, "we should talk about that."

So, we did. I explained, as best I could, how being raped by Kendall had changed Margaret Mary. I talked about how much I hoped I wouldn't like Gianna, only to find out what a nice person and perfect partner she was for Margaret Mary. Dammit.

"Don't swear," My Dad said. "Your mother and I always thought maybe you two would end up together."

"We are together, Dad. Just not in that way."

"I'm glad to hear she's okay and happy and that you are alright with that. Good for you."

I always felt good, better than good, when my Dad told me I had done something right and despite all my abilities to make bad decisions I genuinely felt that with Margaret Mary, I had done something right. But I had not addressed, or even mentioned, the whole Agent Orange no babies thing, not yet; not now. I sensed, rather than knew, this was going to hurt my Dad, probably my Mom too. That conversation would have to wait for another time.

"By the way," my Dad added into the sudden silence, "while you were gone that Emmy girl you were dating called the house a few times. Asked how you were and whether or not you had a phone."

I was kind of surprised to hear this. I never did get around to having a phone in Sierra Blanca and hadn't called or been in touch with Emmy since I left.

"She say how she was doing? Is she alright?"

"She's working out at the Speare House, hostessing. Your mother and I went out there for dinner and she was very nice to us."

"I'll give her a call, you're right, she's very nice."

"Teddy's sister, Connie, has been trying to get a hold of you as well. Teddy's not doing so well. He's been suspended from the police force and is drinking quite a bit. Connie's trying to get him some help, but she says he won't listen. You should go see her."

I would and I did. Later in the day on that sad Christmas morning in Paris I had called home to wish my family a Merry Christmas and tell them I would see them soon. It was then I learned a bit about the extent of Teddy's troubles, which seem to have gotten worse. I was going to give Emmy a call, but I had to see Teddy right away. He's my buddy.

Teddy was apparently holding court every afternoon (and late morning) at the Whipple Café on Merrimac Street. He was now ensconced among the same losers I had walked away from all those years ago. The players hadn't changed. The conversation hadn't changed. The seating hadn't changed. "Permanently Unemployed" Sullivan still wore the same red checkered wool shirt and jeans he had on last year along, comically, with unlaced work boots. He was perched next to Ralphie something or other, bitching about whatever was on the news. The only change I noticed when I came in was Teddy, "among 'em," at the bar, looking terrible.

"Hey Dave! Good to see ya! When did you get back?" Teddy's unshaven, bloated face split into a grin when I came into the Whipple. It was a face that looked like it hadn't smiled in quite a while.

"Yesterday," I answered taking a seat at the bar. Sully and Ralphie nodded at me and went back to their beer. "We need to talk, Ted. Can we go in the back?"

"The back" was the ex-dining room from the days when the Whipple was actually a café. No food anymore, just booze and boozers.

"Sure," Teddy answered, signaling to the bartender. "Charlie, double 7&7, and…what are you havin' Dave?"

"You have any fresh coffee, Charlie?" I asked.

"Fresh four hours ago," Charlie answered a soggy looking cigarette dangling from his mouth.

"I'll have a Coke," I decided and followed Teddy into the back room.

We settled into a booth. Charlie brought the drinks. We were alone in the back.

"Teddy, what the hell happened? You look like shit."

"This gonna' be another lecture?" Teddy answered, taking a big gulp from his drink.

"It's not a lecture Teddy, I'm your friend, remember? What's going on?"

"Nothin's goin' on. I got suspended, that's all." Teddy's reply was surly, guarded.

"That's not all, Ted. I talked with Connie last night. You're separated from Beth, you won't see your daughter, Kevin threatened to kick your ass and you're hanging out here everyday. Did I miss anything?"

"Yeah, you did. I crippled my daughter, fucked up my career, and pissed off about everybody I know, which now apparently includes you."

"I'm not pissed off, Ted, I'm concerned. I care about you and your family. You forgetting we go back a ways?"

Teddy finished his drink in one more large gulp and hung his head. Then half whispered, half sobbed, "I trusted them, Dave. Did whatever they asked…and they poisoned me, they poisoned my daughter."

"They poisoned me too, Ted, poisoned all of us. It's not your fault, it's not mine. We didn't do anything wrong, they did."

"You think knowin' that's gonna' make Samantha get any better?" Teddy's agony had become anger. He yelled for Charlie to bring him another drink.

"What is going to make Samantha get better is the love of her parents, both of them, and all the help we can get from the VA."

"VA ain't gonna' help. I already tried."

"That's why Peter and Cindy and a whole lot of other veteran's groups are suing them. They're trying hard Ted. Why aren't you?"

"It ain't gonna' do any good," Ted growled.

"And this is?" I was raising my voice as well. This was not heading in the right direction. Charley brought the fresh drink. The lightning went out of the air between us.

"I just feel so bad when I look at her, Dave. And Beth too, look what I did to them."

"It's not just you Ted. Can I tell you a story? It's about me and Margaret Mary. I just broke her heart."

Teddy nodded; I had his attention. So, I told him about Paris, about Margaret Mary wanting me to be the father of her child and my refusing to do so. Because of Agent Orange, because of what happened to Samantha, because of what the government did to us.

"I'm not going to have kids, Ted. Not ever. Do you have any idea how honored I felt when Margaret Mary asked me to be the father of her child? And how horrible I felt when I had to say no? We have to fight this thing Ted, hold the government responsible for what they did to us, to all the vets."

"Ain't gonna' do any good," he muttered and downed his drink. He yelled for Charlie to bring him another. "You want another coke?"

I didn't. Teddy gulped the new drink. I could see he was too dug in, too lost in anger and self pity and the alcohol. I got up to leave.

"I'm your friend Ted, always will be. Let me know when you decide to start acting like you deserve it."

"Mass General Hospital. Emergency Room entrance."

Two very surly, bulky guys with broken noses and pistol bulges under their jackets settled into the back of Eddie's cab. Eddie flipped the meter and started driving.

"Somebody you know get injured?" Eddie asked as he wove through the heavy Boston street traffic.

"Guy we just met, maybe," Thug number one answered. Thug number two snickered. Eddie clammed up. Seven minutes later he pulled into the hospital parking lot and clicked off the meter. Neither thug moved. The silence and stillness became very uncomfortable.

"You guys going inside?" Eddie asked, hopefully.

"Nah," Thug number one growled. "You might be though."

Eddie knew what was coming. He had been expecting it. The shakedown. No getting around it in Boston Town. He remained silent, waiting.

"You laid off twenty-two hundred bucks at Milligan's last week and Paddy the Barber tells me you ditched another grand to him." Thug number two was quoting numbers from a tiny notebook he pulled from his jacket, next to his gun.

Eddie's thriving sports book had grown considerably over the past six months. More often now he would lay off large bets with other bookies to keep his risk factor down. His risk factor just got a lot bigger.

"How much?" Eddie asked.

"Grand a month, starting yesterday. Don't make us come looking for you." Thug number one hoisted himself out of the cab. Thug number two dropped a small white business card for a North End garage in Eddie's lap. "Have a nice day," he sniggered and climbed out of the back seat. Eddie put the cab in gear and drove off. He knew the address on the card. Winter Hill, Whitey Bulger territory. Payment was not optional. Eddie needed a new plan. He wasn't the only one. Like the song said…

In my little town
I grew up believing
God keeps his eyes on us all

And he used to lean upon me
As I pledged allegiance to the wall,
Lord I recall,

My Little Town *

Lyrical Aspirations:
My Little Town, Paul Simon

Chapter Eight

Repercussions

"You want to explain to me again why opening up our law office underneath a pool hall is a good idea?" Cindy asked as the desks and file cabinets and office chairs they ordered were being delivered.

"Fudgie's is a Lowell institution, a landmark," Peter replied, "It's been here forever, everybody in town knows where it is."

"Being downstairs from a pool hall is not exactly going to attract the Cadillac trade," Cindy observed.

"Cin, Lowell has very few Cadillacs, but it has lots of guys who play lots of pool and get into lots of trouble. This place is going to be a gold mine I tell ya'."

"I'm the one who has to work in this gold mine. You will be over in City Hall in the well lit, respectable Public Defenders Office."

"Yes, but I will be thinking of you," Peter grinned sliding a desk into place.

"Why do they call it Fudgie's?" Cindy asked. Warily.

Peter became serious. "Cin, trust me, you never, ever, want to know why they call it Fudgie's."

"It smells up there."

Yeah, Peter thought, another reason why you don't want to know why they call it Fudgie's. Changing the subject Peter asked, "Cin, I've got something I want to ask you to do that I know you absolutely, probably don't want to do."

"Do you mean with or without my clothes on?" Cindy smirked.

"I still haven't thought of anything you didn't want to do without your clothes on," Peter replied happily, but added, "No seriously, Cin, I need to ask you a big favor."

Cindy stopped what she was doing, pulled a chair over to where Peter was standing, sat and said, "So ask."

"You like my parents, right?" Peter began, Cindy nodded. "They've put up with a lot from me. I got kicked out of Keith Academy, resigned from the priesthood, went through law school on their dime and asked you to marry me without ever giving them a clue that I was going to."

"You needed their permission?" Cindy asked.

"No, but I would have liked to have had their blessing. Don't get me wrong, they love you and think our getting married is a great idea. They have done so much for me, and for us. I want us to do something for them."

"And that would be?"

"Would you consider getting married at the Immaculate Conception church? Big wedding, country club reception, dance band orchestra? They want this."

"Me? The blushing bride? Wearing white? You in a tux. Best man and bridesmaids? Big organ, big church? Wedding cake. Hokey pokey dancing?"

Peter sighed. He thought so. His parents were going to be very disappointed.

"I'm in," Cindy proclaimed. "Let the festivities commence."

'You mean you'll do it?" Peter was astonished.

"I'll do it for them, I'll do it for you, and I think I'll get a kick out of it myself," Cindy declared.

"Why?" was the only thing Peter could think of to say.

"Peter, I've told you before, I think the whole church thing with flying angels and virgin Mary's and blue-eyed Caucasian Jesus's is ridiculous. The whole thing makes about as much sense as the Wizard of Oz and Superman. But the ceremonies, you call them sacraments, are good, useful, positive. They serve a wholesome social purpose. If it makes your parents happy, if it makes you happy, then it makes me happy. Let's do it!"

"We're going to hokey pokey?" Peter was still stunned.

"We're going to hokey pokey our brains out."

Lawyers in love.

Annie DeShay arrived in Homer three days after Christmas driving a brand spanking new Jeep Wrangler CJ-6 Custom which was worth more than half the houses in the small fishing village. Within one afternoon she had rented LT's old room above the diner, paid cash, unpacked and started asking around town for work. Annie was 28, dressed in clothes as stylish as her Custom Wrangler and vague about everything else. She had green eyes that at one point in her life liked to smile, the face of an angel, the body of a dancer, and the temperament of someone with a lot they did not want to talk about.

"And she's working just for tips?" LT asked Bill Lucier, the VFW afternoon bartender.

"Tips only," answered Bill, "she's a might pretty lady, she won't have any trouble getting tips here."

LT was wondering what other kinds of trouble this newcomer might be. Since settling into his role as town constable LT had begun to look at Homer with a more protective, familial eye. Crime itself was a rare thing, but as Jake Huckleberry's demise proved, shit happens, everywhere.

"You run her plates?" LT asked Luke Drayber, Alaska Highway patrolman and Homer's only other resident lawman.

"No wants, no warrants, plates are clean. Registration comes back Annie DeShay, Santa Barbara, California, as advertised."

"She starts tonight?" LT asked.

"4 PM, Homer's New Year's Eve, Eve Happy Hour," Bill replied.

"I'll come by," LT said.

"Be happy," Bill replied and went back to polishing glasses.

"So, you are the local long arm of the law?" Annie asked when LT made his appearance at Homer's Happy Hour.

"I am," LT admitted, "Actually I'm the town constable and I'm still not very sure of exactly what that means."

Annie had a twinkle in her eye and a grin that was bound to produce lots of tips. "Right now, Mr. Constable, it means you want to know who I am, why I'm here and what I'm up to. Am I right?"

She was, but before LT could say so she said, "And right now I'm telling you that is none of your Goddamn business unless you intend to ask everybody else in this room the same questions or you are going to arrest me." The twinkle was still there, the grin was gone.

"I already know what everybody else in this room is up to. They are decent, honest, hardworking people who welcomed me here not so long ago. I came with my secrets, they have theirs, you can have yours and we all live together as happily as possible. You don't screw that up, I don't arrest you, and by the way, you have beautiful eyes."

The grin came back, but Annie was, at least for the moment, speechless.

That'll give her something to think about, LT mused as he walked away. And a semi-beautiful friendship was begun.

I decided not to call Emmy. I wanted to see her, talk to her face to face, feel what I felt when I saw her, and take it from there. So, I went out to the Speare House, Lowell's high end steak house, where she was working. It was Tuesday night, New Year's Eve, Eve, right around 7 PM. The dinner rush was just over, the New Year's Eve crowd was scheduled for tomorrow night and the place was noisy but calm when I came in.

Now I have to tell you, Emmy always dressed nicely, looked beautiful, but tonight, she took my breath away. She was looking very elegant in a black cocktail dress, perfect make-up, hair and big brown eyes that could stop a footrace. She didn't see me come in, she was taking reservations, chatting up diners and lighting the room up with her smile.

My first thought was, Wow! My second thought was, What the hell am I doing here? You see, Emmy was almost perfect, what any guy would want, should want, in a partner, in a wife. Any employed guy that is, one with a future, and a plan. At this point I had neither.

Undecided what to do next, I took a seat at the bar and waited to catch her eye. Elegant came to mind, gracious, sexy, and the more I thought about this the less certain I was of what the hell I was doing there. Then she saw me, and I saw her seeing me. Her gorgeous smile became even more gorgeous as she rushed across the room. I stood up to greet her and she threw herself into my arms and kissed me, hard.

"You're back!" She exclaimed while I caught my breath. "When did you get back? Why didn't you call me? How long are you home for? It's so nice to see you!" All exploded from her while we held each other, the center of attention in the Speare House cocktail lounge.

"Wait, wait, wait," she said, breaking our clinch. "I'll be right back." She went over to her podium and spoke briefly with another girl who took over her post. As she was walking back to join me, I was struggling to figure out which of her questions to answer first. We took a booth, and I started to explain. I told her I had resigned from the Patrol, didn't know what I was going to do next, had just got back from Paris and that she looked wonderful, not necessarily in that order.

"Paris! You went to Paris! Why! Tell me all about it." She took my hands across the table, and I swam around in her eyes.

I told her about Margaret Mary, everything except the baby thing. She said she remembered Margaret Mary from high school, the smartest girl in her class, cute too. She expressed some surprise about the Gianna part but knew a little about the Kendall situation and the aftermath, which I had told her about before I went to Texas.

"So, you resigned from the Border Patrol, went to Paris to see Margaret Mary instead of coming here to see me and now you are here. Why?"

Like I was ever going to have the right answer to that question. Instead, I tried to explain further, "Em, I've known Margaret Mary since we were kids. She's the best, the kindest, most special person I know. She said she had something to ask me, that I needed to be there with her to answer. That's all I knew when I went to Paris. I want to tell you all about that, but this is not the time or the place."

"And when and where would that time and place be?" She asked, reasonably.

"Whenever you like. I'm staying at my parent's house for now, looking for a job, settling in. You tell me where and when and I'll be there."

"What are you doing tomorrow night?" She asked.

"Tomorrow? New Year's Eve? Not much, nothing actually."

"Then you should come to my mother's house for the party. All the 'barking Greeks' as you call them, will be there. We can stay, or we can go somewhere and talk."

"Are you telling me you don't already have a date for New Year's Eve?"

"I had one, until I saw you. Do you remember Jimmy Polous from high school?"

"Kind of, I think I had a class or two with him."

"Well, he's Doctor Polous now. He's a dentist. He asked me to marry him."

"What did you say?" Suddenly it was very important for me to know.

"I told him I'd think about it and I have. I don't think I want to marry Jimmy Polous, and I am now going to tell him so."

"And he was your date for tomorrow night?"

"He was, or is, unless you are interested."

Jimmy was going to be one disappointed dentist.

"They're squeezing me hard, Charley. A grand a month they want."

Eddie was bemoaning his fate with Charley Shay down at Milligan's Pub.

Charley was not sympathetic. "My tariff's the same," Charley declared, "They are Whitey's boyos they are, and not to be trifled with. You pay, or you don't play."

"And they are wired in with the cops?" Eddie asked.

"They are, and we are not. Such is life." Charley spoke in a voice accustomed to the system. Resigned, realistic, dismayed.

"Know anybody wants to buy a cab?" Eddie asked, more than half seriously.

"A licensed cab, maybe," Charley replied, "Yours? A horse of a different color is it not?"

"What do I gotta' do, Charley? Get out of the business?"

"I'm afraid you are misinterpretin' the grand a month you owe, Eddie my lad. You owe the grand whether you're in the business or not. It's on their books you are now, and they're not carin' how you get their money. The time of the independent player such as yourself has passed, my boy. These Winter Hill lads control the trade and that means they control you."

Whitey Bulger's Winter Hill gang acted with total immunity in the Boston crime community. Word on the street was that Whitey had a rabbi in the Boston police department. They were wrong. Whitey had a childhood friend in the FBI, a crooked, protective, criminal childhood friend. Extortion, numbers, dope on the street, murder and robbery were all on Whitey and his gang's menu. And now Eddie's name had been added to the list.

"I've got to talk to my Ma." Eddie sighed, and my lawyer, my probation officer and a travel agent, he added silently.

"You best be talkin' to somebody," Charley answered, "These boys mean business, Boston ain't what it used to be, but it is like it always was."

Which meant Eddie's life as an independent bookmaker was over. As he reviewed his options Eddie came to realize his future in Beantown was bleak. There weren't enough taxicab hours in a day to cover a thousand dollar a month tariff from the gangsters and his own expenses. Any other action he might conjure would likewise be subject to the squeeze. Eddie came to the only conclusion he could muster; it was time to hit the road again.

At the Whipple Café in Lowell Teddy slammed boilermakers and bitched about life with the other sorry inhabitants. He only had three more days till his suspension was up and he was determined to stay as drunk as possible till then.

"Buncha' shit Staubach throws that pass. The Vikes laid down I tell ya'" Some conversations, most conversations actually, never change at the Whipple.

Only there could a Heisman Trophy winning, Annapolis Graduate Naval Veteran Quarterback like Roger Staubach throw a last-minute touchdown pass to win a playoff game for the Dallas Cowboys with 24 seconds left and still be a "buncha' shit."

"Permanently Unemployed" Sullivan nodded in agreement. Ralphie something or other agreed as well. Teddy ordered another beer. He didn't much care.

"You comin' to the New Year's thing tomorrow night?" Permanently Unemployed Sullivan asked.

"Yeah," Teddy answered, "Got nowhere else to go."

"Why would'cha wanna' go anywhere else anyway?" Ralphie mused while hunched over his beer.

Teddy was not heading for a Happy New Year.

"There are other ways we could have our babies," Gianna said in the sadness of the days following David's departure from Paris.

"It is not just for me, for us, that I am sad," Margaret Mary replied, "but for David as well. I know there are other ways for us, but for him there are none."

"I do not understand how your government could do such a thing to their own soldiers," Gianna wondered.

"And also they have done this to us," Margaret Mary replied sadly.

Gianna sat next to her, put her arms around her. "Tomorrow night we must go to the Champs Elysee to see the fireworks for 'Le Revillion de la Saint-Sylvestre,' New Years Eve, as you call it, then to my sister Lucia's for the feast. There will be fine food, beaucoup de artistes, much dancing and perhaps a perfect father there as well."

"Perfect for you perhaps, for me, not so much," Margaret Mary replied, "but we will dance and there will be the feast!"

And together they vowed to put the old year behind them and start the New Year anew.

"Where's the dentist?" Uncle Vinnie asked a bit belligerently.

I had just made my entrance to Emmy's family New Year's celebration. Emmy worked the Speare House front desk until eleven, then I picked her up and here we were.
"Thio," Emmy laughed, "you remember David?"

"The dentist was going to fix my teeth," Uncle Vinnie responded, getting the attention of Uncles Joe and Paulie, who came over to us as well. All three were staring at me. Emmy held onto my arm, smiling. The uncles were not smiling.

"Away with all of you, and your teeth as well," Emmy's mother Maria, said as she shooed them away. She greeted me warmly with a kiss on the cheek. "My daughter has missed you so," She whispered.

"And I, her," I answered, also in a whisper.

And after a few more welcoming handshakes and hugs I was back in the fold. Apparently, Jimmy Polous had never been referred to by his first, or last names. He was always "the dentist" in conversation and reference.

"Guy wore ten-dollar shoes," Vinnie said, sipping on an ouzo, referring to "the dentist."

"Looked like he had his haircut under a soup bowl," Uncle Joe added to a round of laughter. Apparently, I was a welcome upgrade. So far.

"So, you's been down in Texas, what? Bein' a cowboy?" Uncle Joe asked.

"Border Patrolman," I answered.

"What the hell is a Border Patrolman?" Uncle Vinnie asked, also with ouzo.

"Border Patrol is a Federal Officer. They're a big deal. Very important," A new uncle commented as he joined the inquisition. He was a lot younger than the Vinnie, Joe, Paulie trio, but had the same hale, hearty and hefty look. Uncle Nick, who I had not met before, was three hundred pounds wrapped in a red and blue checkered polyester sport coat that looked big enough to cover a football field. He had pinky rings, gold chains and a snazzy looking wristwatch the size of a pizza on his wrist. His shoes looked like they cost a lot more than ten dollars.

"I'm Nick Kazantoros, Emily's long-lost uncle," He said as he squeezed my hand. Nick, it turned out, lived in southern California, Laguna Hills, and had left Lowell several years before under some sort of a cloud. He had apparently done well in SoCal and was home for the holidays, strutting his stuff.

"Nice to meet you Nick," I answered, freeing my hand from his grip.

"You bein' good to my niece?" He asked.

"Always, Nick, she deserves it."

"Bet your ass she does," Nick answered, "I can't believe how much she's grown up. She was just a little girl when I left here."

Meanwhile the three uncles wandered back to the kitchen where the spanakopita, moussaka and roast lamb awaited. Emmy was in deep conversation with aunts and cousins, though she cast an enchanting look my way whenever possible. Meanwhile I had Uncle Nick.

"I own this big moving company," he explained, "thirty trucks, American Red Ball Movers. We move people all over the world. Got a partner named Mike, he takes care of the books, I take care of the customers, got thirty guys workin' for me."

"Sound like a great organization, Nick, good for you," I answered.

"What chew doin'?" Nick asked, now that you ain't a Border Patrolman no more?"

"Looking for work, Nick. I have an appointment next week down in Boston with ATF."

"What the hell is ATF?" Nick asked, finishing his ouzo and looking around for more.

"Alcohol, Tobacco and Firearms, it's part of the Treasury Department."

"You like workin' for the government?" Nick asked.

"I don't know, I haven't talked to these people yet."

"Hey Nick!" A voice yelled from the kitchen, "You want any of this pita you better get out here!" Vinnie was waving from the kitchen. Nick turned to go. "I'll talk to ya' later, I don't get out there there'll be nothin' left but dirty plates."

Nick left; Emmy arrived. Things were looking up. "Come on," she said, "we can sit in the Front Parlor."

One thing about visiting Emmy's mother's house, NOBODY sat in the Front Parlor. All the furniture in there was covered in thick plastic covers, with zippers. The sofa, two chairs, and a hassock - all were plastic wrapped. Uncles, aunts, nieces, nephews, NOBODY sat in the Front Parlor. We crinkled down on the sofa, in the darkness. Emmy sat very close. She smelled very good. I put my arm around her. Then Uncle Nick snapped on the lights. "Hey, lookit this!" He called out. "I ain't never seen anybody sit in this room before!"

Then there was a crowd of astonished onlookers peeking into the forbidden room. I hurriedly took my arm back from around Emmy and started to stand up. She pulled me back on the sofa. Emmy's mom came into the room, clicked the lights back off and ushered the gawking crowd back into the rest of the house.

"Let's leave them alone," she announced, "I'm sure they have plenty to talk about."

Bless her heart.

Darkness restored, Emmy said, "Margaret Mary, Paris, had to be there when she asked you something, now is the time."

So, I told the tale. I began with the birth of Teddy's daughter, Samantha. Teddy's heartbreak, Beth's heartbreak, my heartbreak. I am very practiced at not letting horrible events get to me. Two years in Vietnam will do that. Samantha's birth got to me.

I told Emmy about my vasectomy. I admitted to her my horror, absolute fear that I would father such a child and be responsible for the debilitation. I didn't go into a lot of detail about the anger in me, the beast I knew slept inside, which I had come to think of as the Kendall monster. But I told her I could never be a father, that I was not brave enough to face the possibility of a disabled child.

Emmy was quiet throughout. I had more story to tell. She knew about my history with Margaret Mary, I had told her before about what happened between her and Kendall and I explained, as best I could, her relationship with Gianna and how I realized it was best for her, and probably for me.

Then I got to Margaret Mary's request, and Gianna's. I tried to explain my answer and how much pain my answer caused. Emmy's eyes got big, bigger actually, and I noticed they were wet with tears. She put her head on my shoulder and whispered, "That is the saddest story I have ever heard." And for the first time I realized how sad it was as well.

Suddenly the parlor lights blazed on again. "Hey you two! Five minutes to New Year! C'mon and join the party!" This guy, Uncle Nick, had incredibly bad timing. I should have paid more attention to that. Emmy and I rejoined the family. The Times Square Ball slid down the pole, Dick Clark wished everyone a Happy New Year and 1976 began. There were lots of hugs and cheek kisses, laughter and ouzo until Emmy said, "Come on, we can go now," and started leading me to the front door.

"Go where?" I asked as she picked up a green shoulder bag and we slipped away.

"Holiday Inn, Tewksbury. I made the reservation from work, and I got us a late check-out."

I told you she was a keeper.

We drank a toast to innocence
We drank a toast to now
And tried to reach beyond the
emptiness
But neither one knew how

We drank a toast to innocence
We drank a toast to time
Reliving in our eloquence
Another auld lang syne *

1976

Lyrical Aspirations:
Same Old Lang Syne Dan Fogelberg

Chapter Nine

Entrees

"**Y**ou are back on the job, Officer Gianoulous and I wish you well, but we will be watching you. You are out of chances."

This was Teddy's greeting as he stood his first roll call after his supension. Teddy had showered, shaved, wore his best unifom and adopted a penitent attitude upon reporting in for his shift.

"Sir, yes sir!" Teddy replied, heels locked at attention, back straight, eyes clear.

Two nights later he was found asleep in his patrol car smelling like stale beer and piss.

"My Uncle Nick wants to take us to lunch tomorrow," Emmy said as we shared a pizza at Rocco's Italiano. Any girl who agrees to split a medium pizza with you and then only eats one slice is a keeper, but I already said that.

"He's going back to California the day after tomorrow. I think he's going to offer you a job," Emm added as she sat back, finished with her share of the pie.

'What kind of job?" I asked between pizza chews.

"With his company I think." Emmy composed herself and looked me in the eye. "Nick is here showing off. He left Lowell five or six years ago as the black sheep of the family. He got into some kind of trouble and had to leave town. I remember he left on a Greyhound bus and nobody talked about what he had done. Now he's doing well and wants the family to know about it."

"What's that got to do with offering me a job?"

"I'm not sure, but he wants us to come out to California and visit. He says we can stay with him and his wife in Laguna Hills, wherever that is, and have a vacation."

"What do you think?"

"I think he's trying to be nice and I thnk he's showing off."

"What do you want to do?" I asked.

"I think we should go to lunch and listen."

So we did.

Haven't seen you around much lately." Bill Egard announced when LT dropped by the VFW Hall two days after the town's New Year's celebration.

"Been up-country a little bit, training the new guy," LT answered bellying up to the bar.

"How's the kid working out?" Bill asked.

"He's smart as a whip, got a degree in biology from up in Fairbanks. Needs a little 'way of the world' smartening up though."

Michael Lewis Armstrong was the new game warden assigned to work under LT by the state Wildlife Commission. He was 23, married, with a two-year-old child. His wife and son were still in Fairbanks while he looked for accommodations for his family in Homer.

"Poachers still working Deep Creek?" Bill asked.

"Not anymore," LT answered. "I've got it pretty well posted now and with the Comber brothers in custody activity has kind of fallen off."

"I heard they took a shot at you," Bill said.

"That's why they're in custody, Bill. Gonna' be there for a while too."

"Good riddance," Bill announced as he placed a coffee, without, in front of LT.

"How's that new girl working out?" LT asked.

Bill hesitated before answering, looking a little embarrassed.

"You might ask her yourself," Annie DeShay said as she stood behind LT.

"You know Bill, this must be the only VFW hall on the planet that doesn't have a mirror behind the bar so a guy can tell when someone is sneaking up on him." LT spun around on his bar stool to see Annie, sparkling and smiling in a red vest, white blouse, tight jeans and cowboy boots grinning his way.

"And if I do sneak up on you it won't be to tell you how I've been doing," Annie announced taking the stool next to LT. "Coffee with, please," she ordered, adding a shot of Bailey's Irish Cream to the mug. "The new girl is doing just fine, thank you very much, and she likes to be called Annie."

"I'm glad to hear that, Annie," LT replied.

"You have anything else to say to the new girl, Officer LT?" Annie asked.

"I was kind of wondering how you would like to go for a boat ride, Annie?"

"Boat ride to where?" Annie responded.

"Along the coast, up Deep Creek ways. You know, around." LT declared.

Why, exactly, would I want to do that?"

"Exactly because if all you ever see of our community is your apartment, this hall and your walk to work, you'll get tired of the place and move on. I wouldn't like that."

"What exactly would you like?" Annie replied, with a hint, just a hint of hostility.

"I'd like you to see how beautiful it is around here, and maybe, just maybe, you'd stay a while longer."

"And that would make a difference to you?"

"It already has," LT admitted, and the boat ride was on.

"We can represent you on an appeal through the police union, Ted, but looking at the statement of charges it doesn't look like we have much of a case." Cindy was speaking across her desk beneath Fudgie's Pool Hall with Teddy. He looked ragged, forlorn and helpless. Cindy looked worried.

"Peter is coming over for lunch, we can have him take a look at this and see what he thinks," She suggested.

Teddy had no words. He had descended through multiple reprimands, suspension and now, termination. Alcoholism was given as the justification for his removal. Cindy knew it went deeper than that.

"I'll need a $1200 dollar retainer to get started," Cindy said, "This is going to require a lot of work on my part, and yours. I want you to come back at 4:30 this afternoon. Peter will be here, and we can strategize what our next move is."

Teddy nodded in agreement, wrote the check, and shuffled out of Cindy's office. He headed straight for the Whipple café.

"I want you'se to come and work for me," Uncle Nick stated between gargantuan bites of roast lamb and garnish.

Emmy and I watched in wonder as Nick packed away the chow. The Olympia restaurant was Lowell's best Greek eatery, but, even so, this guy could gobble some calories.

"Doing what?" was all I could think of to ask.

Nick put down his fork, chewed a moment, and said, "I got these accounts, big companies, you know, like McDonell Douglas and Raytheon. I move their employees when they get transferred. These guys have like, 'transportation managers' who give out the moves. They're all college guys, like you. I need a college guy to talk to these people."

"Doing what exactly?" I asked.

"You know, like takin' 'em to lunch or a ball game or sumthin', whatever it takes to get the business."

I looked at Emmy. She half rolled her eyes, charmingly.

"I don't think I would be very good at 'whatever it takes' and I don't know a thing about the moving business," I answered truthfully.

"You don't have to, I'll teach ya'. Look, why don't you two come out and stay with my wife and me for a coupla' days. We got a big house, lotsa' room. It'll be like a vacation. I'll buy your plane tickets."

I looked at Emmy again. She shrugged her shoulders, gracefully.

"Nick, I really appreciate the offer, and we can buy our own plane tickets. I want to talk this over with Emmy and we'll let you know, Okay?"

"I'm leavin' tomorra'. You should let me know by then." And then he started eating again.

"Well?" I asked as Emmy and I walked back to my car. Uncle Nick had gone to play a round of golf with Uncles Vinnie, Joe and Paulie. There would be a lot of lost golf balls, swearing and at least one golf cart accident.

"I've never been to California." Emmy answered. Neither had I. Our talk continued, our decision was made. Over the hill and far away, once again, vacation or vocation, California here we come.

"I've got a few things to do before I can go," I said. I was not unaware of the troubles Teddy was having and needed to find out how I could best help, and I had a job interview, in Boston, for the Bureau of Alcohol, Tobacco and Firearms. Fabian Crobek, my former roommate Ron's dad, had stepped up to the plate for me after I explained to him why I left the Border Patrol. Fabe was a good man, and he got me a very hard to get interview with ATF.

First things first, then off to California.

"I'm very wealthy," Annie declared as she and LT sat on a blanket overlooking Elk Cove along the Deep Creek waterway. She did not sound proud; she did not sound happy. She sounded sad.

"Aren't we all," LT responded, not understanding the nature of Annie's confession.

They were on the picnic portion of the promised boat ride LT proposed the day before in the VFW hall. The weather had mercifully cleared to a crispy forty-ish degrees, downright balmy for January in Alaska, and they had spent the morning cruising the inlets and coves above and around Homer. They saw gigantic brown bears bellowing, mountain goats gamboling, playful otters playing, industrious beavers building, and something LT had described as a hoary marmot, which Annie had never heard of, marmotting.

Overhead Annie saw her first magnificent bald eagle in the wild, they watched peregrine falcons fishing from on high, and common and not so common thick billed murres waddling, whatever the hell they were. LT pointed out and described each with respect and wonder. In these, he too described himself as very wealthy.

"You don't understand," Annie continued, "My father left me a LOT of money. They say he owned half of Santa Barbra and leased the other half. I've spent my whole life in private schools, academies, touring the world, jet setting, they call it."

"Sounds horrible," LT replied, trying to lighten the mood. It didn't.

"I'm trying to tell you something," Annie declared, "Will you try to listen?"

Mollified, LT shut up. Annie continued, "Anyone who ever met me, anyone I ever met, found out about my money first or inevitably. From that point on I never knew whether it was me, or my wealth, they were most interested in. I've never had a job, never spent a nickel I had to work for, never went without or felt a need I couldn't immediately fill."
"And now you are working for tips in a veteran's hall at the end of the world," LT said, respectfully.

"Now I'm trying to find out who I am without the millions of dollars. I'm trying to find out if people will like me because of me and not my money."

"How's that going so far?" LT asked, cautiously.

"I like the people in Homer. I think some of them like me, I want more of that, I need more of that."

"From what I hear around town you're doing all right so far."

"Am I? I can't tell." Annie's question was filled with hope and despair.

"Look, Annie, I came here with secrets just like you. I worked at staying sober, being reliable, gaining trust. I got through some hard times and here I am. If I can do it, you can do it."

"And I don't sound like I'm playing 'poor little rich girl?'"

"You sound more like you're playing lost little rich girl. You can trust these people, Annie, they are real. You can trust me, I promise."

So, LT kissed Annie and Annie kissed LT back, and all the confusion that inevitably follows, followed.

At 4:30 that afternoon I met Peter and Cindy at Cindy's law office beneath Fudgie's Pool Hall. Teddy was late, frustration was mounting.

"He's in pretty rough shape," Cindy offered as we waited.

"The case against him is strong, multiple infractions, prior warnings, all in writing, eyewitness testimony," Peter added.

I had no idea how far Teddy had fallen. I tried to call him a time or two when I got back from Texas, but he always put me off, said he was working or busy when I wanted to get together. I had no idea of the suspension until I talked to his sister, Connie. This wasn't good.

"What can we do?" I asked.

"I will immediately file an appeal and try to get the police union to back us up. The appeal will at least keep his health benefits intact while being adjudicated. After that, I don't know," Cindy said.

"This isn't Teddy," I offered, "this is what happened to Teddy after Samantha was born, what Agent Orange did to her and what Teddy is doing to himself because of it."

"You believe that," Peter said, "I believe that - what we have to do is get the Lowell Police Department and Teddy himself to believe that."

At which point Teddy stumbled into the office. He wasn't drunk, he wasn't sober either, but he was twenty minutes late and surly.

"Hi Dave," he slurred, "what are you doing here?"

"Tryin'to help you Ted. What the hell happened?"

"Buncha' shit is what happened. They're all just out to get me."

"Ted, asleep in your patrol car is not a bunch of shit, especially two days after coming off a suspension. This is serious trouble," Peter announced as gravely as he could muster. Teddy scoffed, Peter continued, "Here's the bottom line, Ted, if you want us to help you. Ninety meetings, ninety days in AA. You get a sponsor, he signs your court card after every meeting, every day. One week from today you come back here with your sponsor. We talk again. Otherwise, you take back your check and good luck to you."

Cindy was uncharacteristically quiet while Peter laid down the law to Teddy. They had discussed this before his arrival and decided Teddy might take the directive better from a friend (and a man) than from Cindy. Whatever worked, they hoped. Now it was my turn.

"Ted, can I ask you a question?" I began.

"Why? You on their side now?"

"Their side?" This was pissing me off. "I'm here because I'm on your side, Ted. I was with you the night Samantha was born, and I know how heartbreaking that is. I was in Nam the same time you were, and I know how heartbreaking that was, so I know you've got good reasons to be hurt, to be angry, but what the hell good do you think all this anger and hurt is doing you, or your family?"

"I don't have a family, Beth left me," Teddy sniveled.

"I've spoken with Beth, Ted. Several times. She didn't leave you; she left the abusive drunk you've become," Cindy snapped. "I don't know you very well Ted, but these guys do, and they think you're worth saving, but I am not going to work one bit harder at saving you than you will at saving yourself."

Ted bristled. Peter stood up. I got between Teddy and Cindy. Things were tense until Ted deflated, his shoulders sagged, his voice broke, and he sank into a chair.

"I'm lost," he said, "I don't know what to do. I don't know how to feel. I'll do whatever you guys say."

And the tiny office became brighter, lighter, and filled with hope.

"Vegas, Ma, you'll love it!" Eddie was pitching the hard sell. Las Vegas, Nevada, the far side of the moon to a woman born and raised in South Boston, safe haven for a rookie-bookie cabdriver now on Whitey Bulger's deadly radar screen.

"You and me and Auntie Cam, I can get us a nice place, with a porch for flowers, lotsa' sunshine, no snow, air conditioning even!" Eddie was running out of promises. His mother looked skeptical, Auntie Cam looked doubtful, the future looked uncertain.

"And what about Harrison Street?" Camille asked. "I thought we was moving among the fancy folk?"

"It's very noisy over there, Cam. Ambulances and fire trucks and the like. You'll like Vegas a lot better, I promise," Eddie hoped.

"This wouldn't have anything to do with a coupla' customers you drove over to Mass General last Thursday, would it?" Eddie's mom, Hazel asked, knowingly.

Eddie was stunned. You couldn't slip much that happened in Southie past Hazel.

"You don't think I've been talking to Eddie Shay down at Milligan's?" Hazel declared, as Auntie Cam nodded, knowingly.

"It's Bulger and his gang, Mom. Those guys don't screw around."

"Like as if you told me you weren't screwing around?"

Eddie was nonplussed. He knew he had to get out of town, He also knew he didn't want to leave his mother and aunt behind. He also realized this whole mess was his fault.

"I'm sorry, Ma, it was just a few bets, chump change, practically."

"And what would you be doing in this Las Vegas?" Hazel asked.

"Sports book, in a casino, Ma. It's amazing! Everything I do here that's illegal, is legal in Vegas. I know a guy; he knows a guy says I can have a job. No snow Ma, no three flights of stairs, big lunch buffets."

"No Whitey Bulger," Auntie Cam added, helping seal the decision.

"And no 'screwing around.'" Ma added, forcefully.

"Ma, this is Vegas, I don't even know what I could be screwin' around doin' that isn't already being done."

"You'll think of something, sooner or later," Ma proclaimed, correctly.

Now Eddie had to square the move with his probation officer and then they were headed West.

"Jean-Luc is, I think, the one," Gianna announced one week after attending the New Years' celebration at her sister's home with Margaret Mary.

"To be your baby's father?" Margaret Mary replied.

"To be our baby's father," Gianna added.

"You have spoken to him about this?"

"Not yet, first I speak of this to you."

"Why Jean-Luc?"

"He is talented, yes? One of our finest musicians, he is of good temperament, speaks well, and..."

"He is very handsome," Margaret Mary replied.

"All wonderful things for our baby to be," Gianna concluded.

"You would sleep with him to do this?"

"Non, you I sleep with, you only I make love with. For Jean-Luc we would see a doctor to do this."

Margaret Mary pondered the thought. Since the heartbreak of her conversation with David she had thought of little else. Her desire to share a child with Gianna seemed lost forever. Until now, perhaps.

"How will you ask him about this?" Margaret Mary asked.

"We will have him here to dinner, coquilles St. Jacques I think. And some wine, a crème– brûlée, café au lait, then we will ask him."

"And the doctor? How would he do this?"

"Carefully, I imagine," Gianna giggled and Margaret Mary managed a smile, even a giggle herself.

"Then perhaps the doctor could do it twice?" Margaret Mary blushed. And just as it had in a tiny law office under Fudgie's pool hall, thousands of miles away in Lowell, Massachusetts, the room became brighter, lighter and filled with hope.

And a song played...

Little Darling,
It's been a long, sad lonely winter,
Little Darling,
It seems like years since it's been
here.

Here comes the Sun,
Here comes the Sun,
And I say, It's alright. *

Lyrical Aspirations:
Here Comes The Sun, George Harrison

Chapter Ten

Aloha's

"Let's see, college graduate, honorably discharged veteran, two tours in Vietnam, NCO rank at discharge, no arrests, completed Federal Law Enforcement Academy, Los Fresnos, Texas, Border Patrol one year, no disciplinary actions, fluent in Spanish, Dave you're everything we need here at ATF (Alcohol, Tobacco & Firearms) but I can't hire you."

Just when everything was going so well.

I was being interviewed by the Regional Supervisor for ATF in Boston, Martin Edgars. They are the federal agency which regulates the criminal misuse of firearms and explosives, arson, and tobacco and alcohol smuggling. My kind of good times. The Regional Director loved me, up till a minute ago. I couldn't think of a bright way to say why not? So I just said,

"Why not?"

"Hiring freeze," he explained, "I can only hire Hispanic, Black or Female candidates at this time. Federal order." He didn't sound unhappy, he didn't sound disappointed. He sounded disgusted. Then I had a brilliant thought.

"Ferrier is Portuguese," I answered truthfully, "Used to be Ferrara till my grandfather got to Ellis Island. They wrote down Ferrier, he was too intimidated to say anything and Ferrier we became."

"You can document this?" He replied, smiling.

"I can," I replied accurately.

"I think I can make this work!" Now he sounded happy. Folding his hands atop his desk, he leaned forward in his chair and asked me, in his most confidential voice, "I just need to know one thing, Dave. Your answer will remain confidential, between us. What types of drugs did you use in Vietnam?"

And in that moment my potential ATF career ended.

To him, like so many other people, Vietnam veteran meant drug addict, user, abuser or something in one of those categories. Saddly, we were also labeled "baby killers," "losers," "pariahs." Enough was enough.

As calmly as I could I answered, "Sir you could have asked me IF I used drugs in Vietnam, you could have asked me IF I have ever used drugs at all, and I would have answered truthfully that I tried marijuana twice, and didn't like it. But you didn't ask me IF, you assumed I did, and that makes me just another drug addict Vietnam veteran in your eyes. So no thanks, I don't want the job."

He started to reply. I was up and out of the chair. So much for "don't let the kid drive the truck" being my worst job memory. California with Emmy was starting to look better all the time. And, of course I remembered a song…

Well they'll stone you when you walk all alone,
They'll stone you when you are walking home,
They'll stone you and say that you are brave,
They'll stone you when you are set down in
your grave,

But, I would not feel so all alone,
Everybody must get stoned. *

Dylan certainly knew that had nothing to do with drugs.

"You and Annie were looking mighty familiar with one another at the dance last night," Luke Rayburn mentioned over morning coffee with LT at the VFW hall.

"Me and Annie seems to be a mighty popular subject around town these days," LT answered.

"You mean since she moved in with you last week and started parking her fancy jeep next to your not so fancy pickup?" Luke grinned and sipped.

"Yeah, about that time," LT grinned back, happily.

"Things going okay with you two?" Luke asked.

"So far, so good. Annie's got a past, I've got a past. We're tryin to work it out."

"Try hard, she seems like a good lady."

"So I've noticed. Everything doing okay with you?"

"Fine," Luke answered, and then became a bit somber. "LT, I'm born and raised up here. We see a lot of folks come and go. Some stick, as you have, others, not so much. Annie seems like a nice person LT, but she's not a sticker. One day she'll likely leave."

LT took a sip of his coffee and considered. "I get what you're saying Luke. This isn't the life for everyone. Annie's got a lot going for her back in the states, you're right, she probably won't stay."

"I just don't want to see you get hurt too bad," Luke answered.

"I probably will," LT lamented, "but in the meantime I can enjoy the time we have together." He hoped, helplessly.

"Mon enfants shall be magnifique!" Jean-Luc declared, more than half in the bag after the Coquilles St Jacques, two bottles of Pouilly Fusse, cognac and crème– brûlée.

The 'almost a rock star' had arrived for dinner in a purple crushed velvet jacket, paisley neck scarf, striped bell bottoms, pointy boots and perfumed hair. Margaret Mary and Gianna shared a secret smile as they realized he was better dressed than they were.

After dinner there was much conversation eventually highlighted by Gianna and Margaret Mary's proposition of paternity. Jean-Luc was glowing, proud as a peacock as he described his yet to be born offspring.

"And which of you shall be mon premiere amour? The first to bear my beautiful child?" Jean-Luc cooed.

He was about to become a very disappointed daddy candidate. Gianna began to explain the artificial insemination plan. Jean Luc's expression changed from euphoric to horrified. "C'est impossible!" He stammered, alternating between indignant François and halting English. "This is unnatural! Une parodie!" He was almost sober again. "I have sung with the Beatles! Once I danced with Mick Jagger's girlfriend!"

"You sang with one Beatle, Jean Luc, at a house party, and Ringo was very drunk at the time," Gianna recalled as she and Margaret Mary were silently reevaluating their paternal choice.

"Non!" Jean Luc exclaimed, "there must be une rapport sexuel, avec amour, tres bien amour!"

"Amour, yes," Gianna explained, "but not physique, l'amour por la enfant, l'amour du Coeur, of the heart."

Jean Luc was not buying this. Margaret Mary was amused, relieved and silent. Gianna was persistent.

"This can happen in a doctor's office. It is a simple procedure."

Jean Luc was adamant. He was not looking for a plastic cup and a handshake. After some further bickering he took his indignant leave. Gianna and Margaret Mary were marginally disappointed, minimally chagrined and mildly surprised, before they arrived at an inevitable conclusion.

"I think it is going to be more difficult than we thought to find a Frenchman for a father," Gianna mused. They shared a laugh and then split Jean Luc's uneaten crème– brûlée.

"About this baby, our baby," Margaret Mary began timidly, "I think perhaps it is not for me after all, even with the doctor."

"Because of David?" Gianna asked.

"Not just that," Margaret Mary admitted, "If we are to raise a child, I must respect the father, I must love the father, but for now and forever I love only you."

"And I you," Gianna replied. "But 'pour le pere,' what are we to do?"

"For now, I must do nothing. No more Jean Luc's. We must think of another way."

"So, we shall," Gianna agreed as the night sighed on before them.

The Tuesday evening Alcoholics Anonymous meeting started promptly at 7 PM. Ted entered the basement meeting room of the Weed Street Elementary school reluctantly, but on time. He had not had a drink in 24 hours, white knuckling the process out. He went inside with the others and what he found was a circle of metal folding chairs, a rusty looking thirty cup coffee maker, lots of Styrofoam cups and coffee debris and salvation.

As the room filled with people Teddy withdrew into himself. He found a seat in the circle of chairs and stared at his hands. After the others had seated themselves, he heard the opening invocation, ignored the introduction of new attendees and listened, reluctantly. What he heard was raw honesty, painful confessions, sincere remorse, gritty determination and fragile humanity, struggling, yet striving. Though he could not put his thoughts and feelings into words as yet, he left with a tiny, glimmering morsel of hope for his own sobriety and a resolution to keep coming back.

"This your first meeting?" The stranger asked as Ted stood outside the school after the meeting's conclusion.

Ted nodded, lit a cigarette, wishing he was someplace else.

"You don't remember me, do you?" The stranger added.

Ted considered the man. He didn't recognize him.

"We met years ago at the Lowell Auditorium. I was fighting under the name Kid Gallavan. You cleaned my clock."

The light came on for Teddy. He remembered the fight, not the fighter. "Split decision," Teddy said, "You hit hard."

"You hit harder," the no longer stranger laughed, "so are you a friend of Bill W?"

"Who's Bill W?" Teddy asked.

"Thought so," the stranger replied. "My name is Rick by the way. Can I give you something?"

"Depends," Ted answered warily.

"Relax," Tom laughed, "It's a book, what we call the Big Book."

"I'm not much of a book guy," Teddy admitted.

"Neither was I, until I read this one. Why don't you give it a try?" Rick handed Teddy the Big Book of Alcoholics Anonymous. Teddy handled it like he was juggling snakes.

The cover had Alcoholics Anonymous in large letters atop the page.

"Doesn't look very anonymous to me," Teddy observed.

"Skepticism is what got a lot of us here," Rick offered. "I started hitting the booze after I stopped hitting the gym. Felt like a nobody, acted like a nobody, drank like a somebody."

"How long you been coming here?" Teddy asked.

"Four years, ten months, twenty-seven days," Rick answered with a grin.

Teddy didn't understand the grin. "That's a long time," he answered.

"Not long enough," Rick replied, "lots of damage in my debris field."

Ted thought about his own debris field, little Samantha, Beth, his career, his family and really, really wanted a drink, or two, or more.

"Look, I wrote my number in the book," Rick offered, "give it a try and if you want to talk about it, maybe get a coffee or something give me a call."

Rick held out his hand. Teddy shook it and they parted in the night. Teddy drove slowly past the Whipple café on his way home. Slowly, but past.

"Did you find a sponsor?" Cindy asked when Ted returned a week later.

"Kinda', I been going to meetings, Tuesday and Friday and Saturday I went, and I haven't had a drink all week."

"Ted," Peter interjected, "we're not asking you to see how long you can hold your breath, or delay your drinking. We're asking you to get into a program of recovery. That's going to take a lot more effort than Tuesday, Friday and Saturday."

"I ain't drinkin!" Teddy exclaimed.

"You aren't drinking yet, Ted. Sooner or later, angrier or lonelier, you will," Cindy added.

Ted flashed back to Tuesday night's meeting when he drove past the Whipple Café and didn't stop. He remembered how hard that was and knew in his heart he would stop in, sooner rather than later. "There's this guy I met at one of the meetings, he gave me a book to read, the Big Book he called it. It's pretty good. Maybe I could ask him to be my sponsor."

And later that week Ted asked Rick. He said yes.

Emmy and I flew out of Boston's Logan airport on a snowy, blustery, March Sunday evening. Our flight was delayed twice due to the weather and for a time cancellation was a prospect. Eventually we landed at LAX (Los Angeles International Airport to novice travellers such as ourselves) at 11:30 PM. We were a bubbling stew of tired, excited, disoriented and delighted. The temperature was a balmy 74 degrees. A tropical breeze rattled the tops of towering palm trees, the airport was alive with bustling almost midnight travellers and Uncle Nick was waiting for us at the passenger curb in a brand new, shiny silver Lincoln Continental Town car. What could go wrong?

There were hugs and handshakes. We met Joan, Nick's delightful and friendly wife. We glided through rather surprising late night traffic in automotive luxury for the one hour drive to someplace called Laguna Hills. Lots of concrete, lots of cars, lots of anticipation. Seated side by side in the back seat of the big Lincoln, Emmy squeezed my hand. I squeezed back. We were California Dreamin'.

All the leaves are brown,
And the skies are gray,
I went for a walk
On a winter's day,

I'd be safe and warm
If I was in L.A.
California Dreamin'
On such a winter's day. **

Lyrical Aspirations:
**Rainy Day Women #'s 12 & 35*, Bob Dylan (Who else?)
***California Dreamin'*, John & Michelle Phillips

Chapter Eleven

Differences

"Will you please come with me today, I want you to meet someone?" Margaret Mary asked Gianna as they opened their gallery on a sunny Montmarte Monday morning.

"Of course. Suzanne will be here in one hour; she can watch the shop. Does this have anything to do with where you have been mysteriously going this week past when you have said nothing to me?" Gianna teased.

"It has everything to do with where I have been, but until we go, my secret, bien?"

"Your secret? Bien, for one hour."

Sixty minutes later Margaret Mary and Gianna were in the offices of Sister Beatrice of Navarre, headmistress of a Catholic charities organization which sponsored orphaned children from Southeast Asia.

"You must be Gianna Viscoli, whom Margaret Mary tells me is her partner in life?" Sister Beatrice asked without reservation or judgement.

Gianna had been on high alert, experiencing deep dread ever since they had arrived at Margaret Mary's "secret" destination. She hesitated to enter the convent, agreeing only after considerable cajoling from Margaret Mary, a "matter of trust." Gianna had none. Her childhood had been dominated by strict, swatting, sadistic, cruel Catholic nuns. In her home town of Verona a parochial education was the only education and Gianna had endured twelve harsh years of learning by fear, threat and guilt. Her emotional scars ran deep and hidden, until now.

"I am," Gianna answered the headmistress defensively, cautiously.

"Welcome then to our convent. Here we take care of children who cannot take care of themselves. Among our wards we have twelve Amerasian children brought here after the war in Vietnam. Margaret Mary has been coming here to visit them. Would you care to meet them as well?"

Gianna looked quizically toward Margaret Mary, a conversation for later. Margaret Mary pleaded with her eyes. Gianna nodded yes.

The Amerasian orphans were four boys and eight girls. The oldest was ten, the youngest four. All were rescued in the final days before Saigon fell. They had been here, at the convent for a year and half.

The children were playing in a well maintained, orderly courtyard. All except one, a young girl of no more than five years who sat alone and apart on a little stone wall, watching the others play, watching everything. The solitary, sad child brightened only when she saw Margaret Mary enter the playground. She did not rise up, nor did she move from her secluded seat. She smiled the ghost of a smile and waited, silently, as Sister Beatrice led Margaret Mary and Gianna across the playground. The child mostly resembled a small, wild bird caught in a cage, frightened at being locked up, afraid to fly away.

"Bon jour, Huyen!" Margaret Mary called out, hurrying ahead to where the little girl was seated.

The child brightened, a smile lit her face. She remained stone still. Margaret Mary knelt before Huyen and took her tiny hands into hers. At once the child sprang up and threw her arms around Margaret Mary's neck. They held and hugged. Sister Beatrice and Gianna stopped, lengthening the moment.

Huyen rose, never letting go of Margaret Mary's hand and curtsied to Sister Beatrice. The headmistress smiled and stepped aside as Margaret Mary introduced Gianna, "Huyen, C'est mon amie, mon coeur, Gianna."

Huyen said nothing, flashed her special smile and took a step back, partially hiding behind Margaret Mary. Gianna's expression remained curious, stoic, apprehensive.

"Huyen is our shy child," Sister Beatrice explained in perfect English. "She has been with us the longest, almost three years."

"From Vietnam?" Gianna asked.

"From our orphange there, before the fall of course. She was brought to us as an infant, left on our doorstep. We know nothing of her parents, her family, anything really, only that her father appears to have been an American. Such children were treated very unkindly by the Vietnamese. We have several of them here."

"You were in Vietnam?" Gianna asked.

"I was, until the communists drove us out. We were lucky to get out at all. We had to leave behind all of the children we cared for who were not of mixed heritage. One man, a North Vietnamese Major, smuggled us out to the airport where we were placed on a Swiss airliner and flown here."

Margaret Mary and Huyen watched closely as the Mother Superior and Gianna spoke. The child clung tight to Margaret Mary. Gianna approached them and knelt down to look Huyen in the eye. Gianna smiled. Huyen smiled back. Nothing else was said.

"I wiil take Huyen for a little walk and we will wait for you in my office. Perhaps you two would wish to talk alone," Sister Beatrice said as she took Huyen's hand and retreated across the schoolyard.

Margaret Mary and Gianna indeed needed to talk. Gianna sat on the stone wall. Margaret Mary sat next to her.

"We are here because of this child." Gianna was not asking a question. Margaret Mary nodded. "You have affection for this child?" Gianna then asked, knowingly.

"I do," Margaret Mary answered.

"And what are we to do about this affection?"

"Sister Beatrice said she could spend some time at our home, a weekend perhaps," Margaret Mary proposed.

"She said this knowing we are as we are, together?"

"I told her I loved you and that we are lovers."

"And yet she said yes?"

Margaret Mary nodded. Gianna was reevaluating Sister Beatrice. "Then perhaps for a weekend."

And Margaret Mary threw her arms around Gianna and was happy as Huyen would soon be.

Emmy and I were living the dream. Our first morning in Southern California was drenched in sunshine and welcome. We ate breakfast by the pool in Nick and Joan's backyard. The orange juice was fresh, the sunshine was bright, a Pacific breeze wafted through the yard, it smelled like Never-Never Land. Life was good.

"I have a car for you to use," Nick announced, "you should take the day to explore, drive around, get lost, get found, dinner at six. Any questions?"

"Which way to the beach!" Emmy sang. My thoughts exactly.

"You are going to need this," Nick handed me a thick, spiral bound freeway map book called a Thomas Guide which broke down the extensive Los Angeles freeway system and surface streets of Los Angeles and Orange counties. Each page, and there were LOTS of pages, was about a mile square. It was like being handed a one volume encyclopedia, Brittanica of local geography.

"You are here." Nick pointed to a detailed page. "The ocean is there." He pointed to another. "Good luck."

Youth serves. Emmy and I were off on our adventure.

"Do you mind driving, Em. I need to figure out these maps."

Em didn't mind. I figured out the maps and we headed for the magical blue of the Pacific Ocean.

"I think if you turn left here, we will get to the 405 Freeway, south. Yeah, there's the on ramp." I was digesting the Thomas Guide. So far so good. "Couple miles down there's an exit named Crown Valley Parkway. Should go right to the Pacific ocean."

Emmy took the ramp, and we headed south. I noticed when Emmy was concentrating, like now, she stuck her tongue outside the corner of her mouth. Adorable.

As advertised, Crown Valley Parkway ran dead west, straight to the Pacific Ocean. We crested one last hill and there it was, shiny as a jewel, stretching out forever, a postcard in motion. Emmy sighed. I sighed. We were nibbling at the bait.

"It's beautiful," she said. I was thinking along those lines myself.

"Right turn is Laguna Beach, left is Dana Point, pick 'em." I suggested.

Emmy braked at the intersection of Crown Valley Parkway and the Pacific Coast Highway, looked left, then right. She turned left and changed our lives forever.

"It's not what I want to do, it's what I have to do," Annie snapped as she finished her coffee, with, at the Legion hall.

"I thought doing what you had to do is what brought you here," LT answered.

"It's not that easy," Annie replied with resignation and some small sadness, "My father left me a lot of money and with it a lot of responsibility. I was more used to privilege than responsibility and I ran away. Now, I think I must go back, at least for a while."

"I'm going to miss you, Annie, please come back."

Annie's anger, resentment, and spite melted as she considered LT. "You're the first man I've met in ages that looked me in the eye instead of in the wallet. Lucky me, you don't care about my money, but you won't ever leave a small fishing village at the end of the world."

"I thought you liked it here?" LT asked.

"I like you here but it's a big world, I like it too."

"Even the parts without me in it?"

"Yes," she admitted, "even the parts without you in it."

"When?" LT asked softly.

"In the morning, no sense putting this off."

No sense indeed.

"Does this AA stuff work?" Teddy asked Rick Gallavan while meeting for a cup of Lefty's coffee.

"It works if you work it," Rick replied.

"What's that supposed to mean?" Teddy replied, testily. "All I'm seein' at these meetings so far is a lot of stupid sayings and dry drunks."

"If that's all you're seeing you're missing the most important part," Rick replied.

"What? That they're not drinking?"

"No, that they are there, they are trying, they are making an effort. Some of them may not succeed but they are there, at the meetings, trying. They're not in a bar, they're not passed out in their living room. They are there. Where are you?"

Which stumped Teddy. He honestly didn't know where he was or what he was doing, not at the meetings, not in his life. The question scared him right into honesty.

"Nowhere," He admitted in a sunken, defeated voice. He could not look Rick in the eye. He could not look himself in the eye. Not trying was like that.

"Hey," Rick suggested, "You're here. That's a start."

"Start of what?" Teddy snapped. "My daughter getting any better? My life getting any better?"

"Look, Ted, you're not drinking, you're not hung over and miserable, you're here. That's a start."

Teddy mulled the thought. They sipped coffee. There was silence for several minutes until Teddy admitted, "I can't believe I'm not supposed to have another beer for the rest of my life."

Rick laughed. Teddy glared.

"Neither do I!" Rick laughed. "Ted, you don't have to not drink for the rest of your life. You just have to not drink today. Tomorrow, you start over and decide whether or not you will drink that day. One day at a time, Ted, another one of those stupid sayings you've been hearing."

Teddy gave this some thought. Just one day took a lot of pressure off forever. Just one day.

"So, what's your story Rick? How'd you end up in AA?"

"After our fight I won four in a row, two TKO's. I was pissed when I found out you were in the Marine Corps, and I couldn't get a rematch with you. Then I fought some big Polack from Chelsea, and he knocked me out in the third. Full ten count. I couldn't hurt the guy, it was like punching a brick wall, only the brick wall punched back."

Teddy laughed, remembering. "I fought a guy like that at Quantico only he kept dropping his left. I got lucky."

"I got drunk," Rick said, "After the Polack fight, I got drunk, several times. Got lots of attention, pity from the other bar stools, self pity from myself. Got out of shape, lost two more fights and gave up. Lost two or three jobs, a terrific girlfriend, and all my self respect."

"So, what turned you around?" Ted asked, hoping.

"Ice cream truck." Rick laughed, remembering, then not laughing "I was driving an ice cream truck, and I crashed it. Two o'clock in the afternoon in a neighborhood full of kids. I drove drunk right into a tree. Apparently, I wasn't going very fast when I passed out, but I woke up to a lot of cops and a circle of little kids laughing at me. The cops weren't laughing. Made all the papers, front page. I spent ten days in jail, should have been more." Rick was very far from laughter now. "When I got out of jail, I was ashamed, embarrassed, angry, and hopeless."

"So, what did you do?"

"I got drunk what else?"

Both of them laughed, sort of, in regretful recognition.

"Couple days after I got out of jail again, I woke up in Tewksbury State Hospital. I was handcuffed to the bed; a cop was in the doorway. Somebody had beat the shit out of me. I had no idea how I got there."

"You get arrested again?"

"Nah, they had some mercy on me. Getting the shit kicked out of you isn't against the law. The cop in the doorway was a good guy. He suggested AA, took me to a meeting, saved my life."

Ted thought about this, then asked, "So AA worked?"

"It works if you work it," Rick grinned, "but I already said that."

"Please, please, please, be on your best behavior," Peter implored as he and Cindy waited in the office of Father Scanlon at the rectory of the Immaculate Conception church in Lowell. "He only wants to ask us a few questions about our getting married, we need this, I need this, OK?" Peter added.

The wicked smile Cindy returned normally was all Peter ever needed in reply but this time, this place, he needed more. "I will be good, Peter, for you, for your Mom and Dad, for us…but you owe me." She grinned.

"Father Scanlon is a nice guy, I like him a lot. He was one of the few people who tried to understand why I resigned from the priesthood without making a lot of judgements."

"Well, there was me," Cindy grinned. She was making Peter squirm, then decided to stop that as Father Scanlon entered the room.

"Good afternoon, Peter, Miss Cassen, I presume you are the young lady who has won Peter's heart?"

There was something in the tone of Father Scanlon's voice, a warmth, a sincerity, that immediately won Cindy over. Her cynicism gave way to his charisma and, despite a backlog of cynicisms she was charmed by the man.

"I am." She found herself cooing before becoming irritated with herself for giving in so easily.

"Wonderful," he said, gently taking Cindy's hands into his. "Why don't we sit and talk about this for a while."

Which they did, resulting in a planned High Mass, a reception at the Vesper Country club and Father Scanlon's offer to officiate at the ceremony himself.

As they stood to leave Cindy asked, "Do you by any chance do the hokey-pokey Father?"

Peter cringed, Father Scanlon smiled. "Actually, I do a rather mean hokey-pokey, if I do say so myself."

"I'll save you a hokey," Cindy grinned. Peter sighed with relief and they departed, delighted.

Drifting south on Pacific Coast Highway Emmy and I marvelled at the Pacific Ocean blue of the sea and sky, the swaying, sultry palm trees that lined the roadway, the stuccoed adobe of the beach front housing and the California-ness of the whole scenario. She was smiling, I was smiling. The bait was looking better all the time.

"Let's take a look at this place," I suggested as we came upon the fluttering "Now Renting" pennants fronting a brand spanking new apartment complex overlooking the ocean. Emmy pulled into the freshly manicured parking area facing the clubhouse/rental office of Sea Breeze Apartments. There were sixty-four split level townhouses dispersed around manicured grounds and individual car ports. Inside the management office we found there were three rental models. We looked at them all. Two bedrooms, ground floor, near the pool, across from the beach, $350 a month. One year lease. $250 move in allowance. The bait was shimmering. Time to talk turkey with Uncle Nick.

"Ya' gotta' make an honest woman outta' my niece," Nick proclaimed as we bobbed in his backyard jacuzzi that evening. He was puffing away on a $5 cigar. Emmy was helping Joan prepare dinner. I had never been in a backyard jacuzzi before. Nick and I were doing the man to man thing. The "honest woman" condition came as a surprise. Emmy and I had never talked marriage, we were not even engaged.

I briefly wondered if she knew anything about this requirement and immediatley decided she didn't. Not her style, not mine either.

"Nick, are you saying if I don't marry Emmy I don't get the job?"

"I'm sayin' you do the right thing, I'll do the right thing."

Nick had offered me good money to come to work for him, along with a company car, an expense account, and use of the company's four season tickets to the California Angels baseball team. There was also Sea Breeze apartments, the cobalt blue of the Pacific Ocean, swaying palm trees and no snow. But marriage?

"Nick, I don't even know if Emmy wants to marry me," I countered.

"Look," Nick declared, "Vinnie told me she had the football player boyfriend who is in prison, some dorky dentist with ten dollar shoes and a coupla' guys who weren't around very long. She ain't gettin' any younger and so far you're the pick of the litter."

I was trying to decide whether to be flattered, amused or outraged. I chose amused. This would make for interesting conversation for Emmy and I. But first things first. We had four more days of vacation in Southern California. Disneyland beckoned, Hollywood beckoned. Sea Terrace Apartments beckoned.

Emmy waved from the kitchen to tell us dinner was ready. Adorable. Nick snuffed his cigar out in the jacuzzi bubbles. And somewhere in my head the Beach Boys sang…

Wouldn't it be nice
If we could wake up
In the morning when the day is new

After having spent the night together
Holding each other close the whole night
through...

Oh, we could be married,
And then we'd be happy.
Oh, wouldn't it be nice *

Lyrical Aspirations:
**Wouldn't It Be Nice?* Brian Wilson

Chapter Twelve

Promises

"David! I've been so worried about you! I called your house, and your mother told me you were in California!" Margaret Mary sounded surprised, a little angry and somewhat concerned when I called her after the California adventure. This was going to be one doozy of a phone call. I had been putting it off for a week, then two. Emmy and I had THE TALK, we were going to get married. Now I had to tell Margaret Mary.

Of course, there was no logical reason why I should be reluctant to tell Margaret Mary I was getting married. But I was. The $7 a minute trans-Atlantic telephone silence echoed for about $9 worth before I cleared my throat and asked, "Do you remember Emmy Kazantorus from high school?"

"Of course I do," Margaret Mary answered, "Very pretty, very popular. I hated her until I found out what a nice person she was."

"I'm going to marry her."

About ten dollars worth of trans-Atlantic silence followed.

"Marry?" The haunting whisper from across the sea asked.

"Yes, next Saturday. We are going to live in California."
The trans-Atlantic silence costs were rising. I didn't care,
Margaret Mary didn't notice.

"Do you love her?" I clearly heard the quiver in Margaret
Mary's voice.

Truth be told I wasn't sure. The discussion between Emmy
and I was more like a business deal than a romance. We got
along together just fine, we both wanted to live in Southern
California. I took Uncle Nick's job offer, we signed a lease
for Sea Breeze apartments, we drove the company car,
mastered the freeways, swallowed the bait.

"I better, I'm marrying her."

"That's not an answer, David." Margaret Mary's tone was
troubled, but insistent.

"I think I do, Mags," I answered weakly.

"I think I love someone is not a good place to launch a
marriage," She scolded.

"I like being with her, she's very pretty, she understands
about the no children thing, there's only one thing wrong,
and I can't do anything about it," I answered not sure who I
was getting upset at, but getting mad.

"And what is that?" More maddening patience from
Margaret Mary.

I started, stopped, didn't say anything, and then, before my
seldom used common sense filter kicked in, I blurted, "She's
not you!"

The next silence was a long one.

"I'm sorry, Mags, I didn't mean to say that. I'm really happy that you are with Gianna. I'm happy you're happy. I'm just trying to get the same way."

I could hear Margaret Mary crying on the other end of the phone, an Atlantic Ocean away. The next thing I heard was the choked and saddened voice of the most important person in the world to me say, "Oh, David, I never thought it would turn out this way, did you?"

Imagining the way things would turn out was never a strong point of mine. I had fantasies, daydreams, promises of a world a lot less complicated than I had been prepeared for, and standards I was never sure I was going to be able to meet. But realistic expectations of how things would be, should be, not so much. Stay alive till the end of the day, don't bleed, don't get hurt, try not to hurt anybody else, these thoughts were the best I could manage. And now I listened to Margaret Mary sobbing thousands of miles away.

"It's alright, Mags, I'll be okay, you're already okay and no matter what happens we'll still be friends, right? You and me, us, that will never change. I promise."

Which was a half-hopeful, half doomed prediction, only, mercifully, neither of us had any way of knowing that yet. And of course when I hung up the phone there was a song painfully drifting through my head, recalled from nowhere…

And when we're dancing, it almost feels the same,

I have to stop myself from whispering your name.

She even kisses me like you used to do,

She's everything a man could want

But she's not you. *

It's enough to make me stop listening to the damn radio.

"I ain't powerless over alcohol! I'm not drinkin' now am I? I haven't had a drink in almost two months!" Teddy proclaimed. Rick listened patiently and replied.

"That's great, Ted. You look better, you sound better. How much control over alcohol did you have when they found you drunk and asleep in your patrol car two days after your suspension was over?"

Teddy hung his head in shame, remembering not just that night but all the others, when he hadn't been found out.

"Powerless over alcohol doesn't mean powerless over your life, Ted. Sixty days without a drink is powerful, sixty meetings in sixty days is powerful, being here right now is powerful. For you, and me, and a lot of other people like us, alcohol is what takes away that power. Ted, I've been in a boxing ring with you. I know what you look like when you are focused and determined. That's powerful. Don't you want to start feeling that way again?"

"I'm a little too old to start boxing again," Teddy answered.

"Shit Ted, you get dried out and back in shape I'm going to be wanting that rematch we never had."

Teddy smiled, remembering when and hoping it could be that way again. "So, these 12 Steps things, I gotta' do 'em all?"

"All or nothing, Ted, let's get to work."

THE TWELVE STEPS OF ALCOHOLICS ANONYMOUS

1. We admitted we were powerless over alcohol – that our lives had become unmanageable.

2. Came to believe that a Power greater than ourselves could restore us to sanity.

3. Made a decision to turn our will and our lives over to the care of God as we understand him.

4. Made a searching and fearless moral inventory of ourselves.

5. Admitted to God, to ourselves, and to another human being the exact nature of our wrongs.

6. Were entirely ready to have God remove all these defects of character.

7. Humbly asked him to remove our shortcomings.

8. Made a list of all persons we had harmed and became willing to make amends to them all.

9. Made direct amends to such people whenever possible, except when to do so would injure them or others.

10. Continued to make a personal inventory and when we were wrong to promptly admit it.

11. Sought through prayer and meditation to improve our conscious contact with God as we understand him, praying only for knowledge of his will for us and the power to carry that out.

12. Having had a spiritual awakening as the result of these steps, we tried to carry this message to alcoholics, and to produce these principles in our affairs.

Teddy had a lot of work to do.

"The phones are ringing off the hook! I need you to get over here right away!" Cindy shouted into the phone.

Peter who was at his desk at the Public Defenders office winced, listened, explained, "Cin, I've got fourteen cases on my desk right now. Eleven of them, coincidentaly, claim they are innocent, the other three are in the hospital because they were shot by the police while committing a crime they say they didn't commit. I'm sorry, right away is not going to happen. What the hell is going on anyway?"

"Horatio called from Baltimore. Apparently a TV station in Baltimore ran a documentary called 'Agent Orange, The Deadly Fog.' Baltimore picked it up from Chicago and Channel 5 in Boston is running it this afternoon. 'H' is giving our phone number as the New England contact for veterans. I've had over a hundred calls already this morning."

"I'll be right over, my innocent clients are going to have to wait. See if you can get hold of Dave and Teddy, they can help out on the phones."

I already have, Teddy's here, Dave is on the way."

"So am I, see ya."

Teddy was writing as fast as he could. "I need your full name, service number, and the unit you were with in Vietnam." He scribbled the info as fast as he could, told the caller he would be back in touch as soon as possible and answered another ringing line. Peter rushed into the office with Dave close on his heels. Cindy breathed a sigh of relief and directed, "Dave, take this phone, name, rank service number, good phone contact and we'll call back. Peter, 'H' needs you to call him as soon as possible. I gotta' figure out how to get more phone lines in here."

Within an hour Cindy had the office phone at Fudgie's patched into the law office phones with Fudgie himself taking names and numbers. Peter had to use a pay phone to call 'H' in Baltimore. Cindy was now busy having the phone company install four more phones in the law office. Everything else was a house on fire.

"This thing is dynamite!" 'H' explained. "I've had over five hundred calls in two days since the documentary ran here, and now it's headed your way. Have you ever heard of a guy named Paul Reutershan?"

Peter hadn't, "H" continued. "He was on the Today show this morning, had me in tears. Call the station get a tape. You got enough help?"

"Cindy's working on it, we'll be okay. What do we do next?"

"I'm working on it," "H" explained, "for now just get us names, get them registered. Do good work."

"We will," Peter answered, and they did.

The Legacy of Paul Reutershan

"I died in Vietnam, but I didn't even know it."

Specialist Paul Reutershan was a helicopter door gunner in Vietnam. His duties included flying low level cover for C-130 transport planes who were spraying dense jungle areas with a defoiliant known as Agent Orange. Paul recalls huge swaths of dead jungle, black and lifeless after spraying. Paul's helicopter flew through dense clouds of the deadly mist which they had been assured was non toxic to humans and animals. They were lied to. All the troops in Vietnam were lied to. Agent Orange was lethal, deadly not only to plants but to the tens of thousands of soldiers and Vietnamese civilians who were exposed to it. The Department of Defense eventaully, very reluctantly, revealed that over ELEVEN MILLION gallons of Agent Orange were dispersed onto Vietnam's jungles, villages and US firebases.

As a helicopter crewman Paul was exposed daily, in the air he flew in, from the water he drank, in the bed he slept in. He was first diagnosed with pancreatic cancer in 1978. He died from that cancer that same year. Before his demise he teamed with fellow Vietnam veterans Frank McCarthy and Jimmy Sparrow to form a non profit called Vietnam Veterans Agent Orange Victims. It was the genesis of a nationwide lawsuit which finally culminated in a $250 million dollar settlement from chemical companies like Dow Chemical and Monsanto who manufactured and marketed this deadly poison.

The awarded funds were eventually distributed to the thousands of veterans who took part in the nationwide class action suit. In the terms of the settlement agreement Dow Chemical and Monsanto, primary manufacturers of Agent Orange, were allowed to disavow any corporate responsibility for the damage caused by Agent Orange.

Let justice prevail.

LT watched the giant brown bear lumber down the riverbank, dunk her head into the water and emerge with a flapping salmon which she threw over her shoulder to the three cubs behind her. She dunked again and again, more salmon appeared, the cubs and mama bear ate well. He watched an osprey circle above, dive and fly off with yet another salmon, home to its nest and its dinner. Only hours before LT had run a trio of poachers off this stretch of river, a spawning area safeguarded and posted for trespassers. Earlier that morning he had helped his deputy, Mike Armstrong, clear a beaver dam from a creek better left flowing, much to the consternation of the beavers. They would build elsewhere. The creek would flow free. LT still couldn't believe he got paid to do this stuff.

"You hear anything from Annie?" Mike asked as they drove back into Homer.

"Not a thing," LT answered, "I guess she's pretty busy down there."

"Aren't they all?" Mike said, "That's why I live up here."

Me too, thought LT, though his heart ached for Annie.

Huyen sat at the hand painted, French Provincial Baby Grand piano Margaret Mary had gifted Gianna on her last birthday. Nestling in the sunlit corner of their parlor Huyen watched Gianna's hands as they danced across the keyboards.

"C'est facile, simple," Gianna said while playing the tranquil tune. "Now you try," Francoise and English combining in tuneful conversation. Huyen placed her tiny fingers just above the keys. Slowly at first, then more confidently she pecked out the tune. Margaret Mary applauded, Gianna joining in. Huyen smiled, something she was learning how to do more and more each time she spent a weekend with Margaret Mary and Gianna.

This was Huyen's third weekend visit. Sister Beatrice had come to the apartment several times. The topic of adoption had come up gradually and then earnestly. Sister Beatrice asked Margaret Mary and Gianna to carefully consider their request and with her approval the headmistress was sure the adoption would be arranged.

"This child has blossomed since you came into her life. She has come to love you both very much. I understand that you share her joy, I am confident you can appreciate the responsibility of raising her." Sister Beatrice had become a friend, just as Margaret Mary and Gianna had become patrons of the orphanage. A fund raiser at La Premiere Impression II raised over a thousand francs for the orphanage. Gianna learned that according to the World Health Organization approximately 500,000 Amerasian children were left behind in Southeast Asia after the Vietnam War. These children whether blond haired or blue eyed, dark skinned or curly haired were shunned by the Vietnamese people, often abandoned in orphanages or left on the streets to beg for their existence. The new communist government closed all the parochial orphanages in the country and sent the orphans to work farms or at 're-education centers.' International efforts to rescue these children were minimal and frustrated by the communist bureaucracy. Huyen had been lucky to get out, even luckier now in the care of Margaret Mary and Gianna.

Margaret Mary and Gianna signed the official papers of adoption on Huyen's unofficial sixth birthday. No one knew the actual date of her birth. February 14th was chosen as a feast day of love. There was cake, there were presents, there was joy and happiness.

"Is it possible for us to give Huyen a new first name?" Margaret Mary asked before the signing. Sister Beatrice asked why.

"I have learned that Huyen means jet black in Vietnamese. Gianna and I would like to name her Thanh, which in Vietnamese means bright and sunny, a thing of precious value."

"And what does Huyen think about this change?" Sister Beatrice asked.

"Mostly she just smiles," Gianna said, and the change was made.

"It's a condominium, Ma," Eddie explained.

"What the hell is a condominium?" she replied.

"It's like an apartment, only we own it." Eddie continued, "You'll like it Ma, it's got three bedrooms, a big patio, there's even a pool."

"How much does it cost?" Auntie Cam asked skeptically.

"Don't worry about it, we can afford it." Eddie was selling hard, his mother and aunt weren't buying.

"It's hard to not worry about a thing when you tell us not to worry," Ma added.

"Ma, I got us here didn't I? We're temporarily living in a very nice casino. You and Cam are tearing up the keno parlor and destroying the buffett. I even heard you were cavorting around the pool with an older gentleman the other day," Eddie teased.

"Cavorting is it? I was not!" Ma responded as Aunt Camille smiled in agreement with Eddie.

"Anyway, your furniture will be here in a coupla' days and we can move in to the condominium. As soon as we do I'm gonna' start a regular shift at the sports book. You two can live by the patio and the pool. It's all good, Ma," Eddie pleaded.

"As good as it was when those Winter Hill bums moved in on ya'?" Ma asked.

"That's all behind us now, Ma, I promise. I'm legit now and doing all the stuff that used to make me illegit. Go figure."

Three days earlier Eddie, his mother and aunt arrived on United flight 571 from Logan Airport to Las Vegas, Nevada. For Eddie's mother and aunt, ages sixty-one and sixty-four respectively, it was their first plane ride, the first time either of them had been out of New England. Enchanted as they may have been by their new surroundings, South Boston was in their blood, Las Vegas wasn't. Not yet.

"Ya' did the right thing on that China Rose situation," Eddie's new boss at the Golden Palace Casino, Max Mecham, told him upon their arrival, "You do the fight thing, we do the right thing."

Eddie was offered a position in the Palace's Sports Book. Vegas odds, house edge, temporary room and board, and an inside track to a condominium deal for him and his family. Eddie was all in, with both hands. Now for Ma and Aunt Camille.

"I got us tickets, Ma, Sinatra at The Sands, day after tomorrow." Eddie was playing his ace. Ma was stunned into silence. Camille was overjoyed. Vegas was looking much better to two sisters from South Boston and a practically reformed bookie.

By the end of that first day of Agent Orange telephone calls Teddy was in tears. Sorrowful tales of miscarraiges, still births, rare cancers and horrific birth defects filled three pads of paper in front of him on the desk. He wept for them. He wept for his daughter Samantha. He wept for Beth and for himself.

He staunched his tears with rage, softened his rage with determination of purpose and vowed to do everything he could to right this wrong and to repair his shattered marriage and splintered parenthood.

"You okay Ted?" Peter asked as he found Ted slumped red-eyed and silent before the jangling telephones late in the afternoon.

"Yeah," he mumbled, "No," he admitted, meeting Peter's eyes with soul numbing sadness. Peter pulled up a chair next to Ted.

"Let's take a break, Dave and Cindy can handle the calls for a while," Peter suggested. "Cin, Teddy and I are going to get some fresh air, alright?"

Cindy nodded, phone pressed to her ear, writng furiously. Dave noticed but said nothing.

Ted and Peter took a walk along Lowell's Central Street. They passed the empty lot which used to be The Strand theatre where long, long ago three kids named David, Teddy and Margaret Mary stood in line to see Davy Crockett, King of the Wild Frontier. The familiar brick facades of Newton's Beauty Academy, Martin's Clothiers, and other small, enterprising businesses were reminders of years past and a changing future.

"You're being pretty hard on yourself, Ted," Peter suggested.

Teddy was silent at first, swallowed hard and croaked, "I've messed things up pretty bad, haven't I?"

"Haven't we all at one point or another, Ted?" Peter sighed, "Remember when I was going to be a priest?"

"I didn't know how to ask you about that," Teddy admitted.

"Well, I went off to do something I was sure was right. I did all I could to follow that path, to become a good priest." Peter stopped talking, stopped walking, remembering.

"What happened?" Teddy asked.

"I was sent to Rome, Ted, to the Vatican. That was an honor, a distinction I never imagined having, and it destroyed my desire to be a priest."

"I don't understand," Teddy admitted.

"Neither did I, Ted. Not at first. The Vatican in Rome is a huge palace. The wealthiest, richest in the world. The bishops and cardinals and popes and priests who live there live like royalty, like princes. Fabulous wealth, uncountable treasure, total immunity from any law or government. It didn't feel very Christ-like."

"But don't they do a lotta' charity stuff?" Teddy asked.

"Millions in, thousands out. It's a racket, Ted, at least at the top levels. Here, like at the Immaculate Conception, Father Scanlon and the rest of the priests are good guys, doing good work, but the more I learned about the Catholic Church's leadership and history the less I could be part of it."

"Kind of like the Marine Corps," Teddy realized.

"How so, Ted?"

"The grunts, the men I was with in the field were the finest I've ever known Peter. We believed in our mission, we believed in each other. But some General, somewhere gave his approval to spray us with stuff that could kill us, kill our families, destroy our children. Destroy my daughter."

"And how were we to know those things?" Peter asked.

Teddy had no answer. Neither did his country.

Emmy and I exchanged "I Do's" in front of a Justice of the Peace on the last Saturday in February. My parents were there, Emmy's mother, sister and a herd of Barking Greeks were there, Teddy, Beth and Samantha were there. Cindy bemoaned the absence of the hokey pokey ritual while Peter breathed a sigh of relief. The reception at Emmy's mother's house featured roast lamb, mousaka, pita, pastichio, lots of Metaxa and good wishes. We spent the night in the same Holiday Inn we had spent last New Years Eve in and left for our honeymoon drive to California and a new life on Saturday morning.

The radio played…

We've only just begun to live
White lace and promises
A kiss for luck and we're on our way
We've only just begun. **

Or so we hoped.

Lyrical Aspirations:

She's Not You, Jerry Lieber, Mike Stoller and Doc Pomus
**We've Only Just Begun*, Paul Williams

Chapter Thirteen

Arrivals

"Additionally, there is a sixty-unit apartment complex in Laguna Niguel, "Sea Breeze Apartments" that your father owns and is currently being run by our in-house management company."

Annie DeShay listened carefully while Carl McAdams, her father's legal attorney, listed the properties she had inherited and currently owned. There were many more than she thought, many more than she needed. Many.

"Anything else?" She asked.

"That's it," Carl responded, "though it wouldn't hurt if you visited a few of these sites, showed the colors so to speak. It would make the transition from your father's management to yours a little smoother."

Annie sighed, resignedly. It was not that she did not appreciate, with tremendous gratitude, the bounty her father had willed her it was the responsibility, the mind-numbing financial obligations, the all-consuming maintenance of such wealth that she resented. All the while she listened to the roll call of assets, now her property, her mind kept wandering to the VFW hall in Homer, Alaska, her full tip jar on the mirror-less bar, coffee with, and a Vietnam veteran game warden and town constable named Bob "LT" Baker.

"I'm going down to LA this week. I will stop by the airport office and drive down to Laguna Niguel as well," Annie agreed.

The big, wide world was about to get a little smaller.

"And I would add, Your Honor, that Mr. Mahoney has accepted full responsibility for his actions and expressed sincere remorse for his infractions," Cindy Cassen offered in summation in Lowell District Court.

Temporarily assigned Lowell District Court Prosecutor Peter Rayburn interjected, "Your Honor, I would like to point out that Mr. Mahoney expressed his sincere remorse and personal responsibility only after crashing the 1971 Pontiac he had stolen into a light pole on Lawrence Street, taking a swing or two at the police officer who extracted him from the wreck and blowing a blood/alcohol test at almost three times the legal limit."

Cindy glared at Peter who didn't dare smirk or smile as he addressed the judge.

"The car was being driven without permission, Your Honor, not stolen," Cindy responded.

"Your Honor," Peter added, "When Miss Tanguay decided to amend the original report of the theft of her car she was made aware that she could be held liable for filing a false police report and decided to let her original statement stand in evidence."

"Enough," Judge Larkin decided. "Mr. Mahoney, this is, I believe, your third arrest for driving under the influence is it not?"

Timmy Mahoney nodded his head as humbly as possible making no eye contact with the judge.

"And your license was suspended at the time of your present 'infraction' as Ms. Cassen described it?"

Another humble nod from Timmy.

"Well, Mr. Mahoney, I am not going to further suspend your license, I am going to permanently revoke it, and for that 'couple of swings' you took at Officer Langtane you are going inside for sixty days."

Timmy's knees buckled and he looked helplessly at Cindy. It was now Peter's turn to look humble. Cindy started to speak and was cut off by Judge Larkin. "I am however going to give you credit for the twenty three days you spent in the hospital as a result of Officer Langtane's having to defend himself from your aggression. Your sentence will be followed by two years probation and any further 'infraction' on your part, if you are caught driving an automobile anywhere in the state of Massachusetts or elsewhere, you will go inside for two years. Do you understand me?"

Timmy understood. Cindy fumed. Peter kept looking humble. Timmy was handcuffed and led away. Cindy snapped closed her briefcase and left the courtroom without looking at Peter.

"Mr. Rayburn, would you approach the bench," Judge Larkin said.

"My understanding is that Ms. Cassen is your fiance, is that so?" The judge asked.

Peter nodded. "Then I would suggest you catch up to her and buy her a very nice lunch. Good luck, Mr. Rayburn."

Let Justice Prevail.

The first things Annie noticed about Sea Breeze apartments was that the grounds were clean and well cared for, the tenant's cars, sheltered in car ports, looked newish, and the manager, Terry Trent, was as gay as a basketful of butterflies.

Terry was also an excellent site manager. The books were all in order, there were no outstanding repair requests and the tenants Annie passed and met all seemed happy. Forty seven of the sixty units were rented, the remainder were spotless and open for inspection. Annie was pleased and ready to go.

"Thank you so much Terry. You are doing an excellent job. I am glad we had a chance to meet." Annie was ready to head back up the coast to Santa Barbara, even readier to head WAY up the coast to Homer, Alaska.

"Don't you want to see the tenant list?" Terry pleaded. "I have it right here."

Annie couldn't think of any good reason she needed to see the teneant list, but did not want to disppoint Terry who was waving it proudly in front of her.

"Of course," Annie agreed, taking the list and scanning it semi-carefully. Which is when the name of the tenants in Unit 12 caught here eye. "Here, the Ferriers in 12, do you know where they are from?"

"Of course," Terry twittered. "David and Emmy, they are from New England, Boston I think. I can look it up on their lease papers."

"No, no, that won't be necessary. What can you tell me about them?"

"David is a little gruff, but Emmy is a treasure. She has the most beautiful collection of ear rings!"

"Ear rings?"

"And shoes, oh my god, they're fabulous!" Terry was abviously smitten with Emmy, or at least with her wardrobe.

"Would they happen to be home?" Annie asked.

"Let me look. Emmy's car is in her space. David left for work hours ago."

"Would you mind introducing me to Emmy? I think we may have a mutual friend."

Terry brightened. "Of course! Wait till you see her shoes!"

Emmy answered the door dressed to the nines, as she always was.

"Emmy!" Terry gushed, "You look wonderful! Can we have a word with you? This is Miss Annie DeShay, she owns the joint!"

"I hope we haven't caught you at a bad time Mrs. Ferrier. Are you on your way out?"

"No, not at all. Please come in."

Emmy led them into the spotless apartment. Annie couldn't help herself; she checked out Emmy's shoes. They were fabulous. A sleek Siamese cat gave them a curious once over and went back to her personal grooming. Emmy motioned to the living room and asked if they wanted something to drink.

"Do you have any of that delightful mint tea we had the other day?" Terry asked.

"Peppermint," Emmy said. "Of course, two?"

They nodded, Emmy served. Annie began.

"Did your husband go to UMass a few years ago?" Annie inquired.

"Yes, he graduated in 1975."

"Did he ever mention a roommate named LT, or Bob Baker?"

"He did! Dave said he ran off to Alaska or something. Do you know him?"

"I lived with him for a couple of months up in Homer, Alaska. He's a state game warden there and the town's constable."

"David will be so happy to know. He said his roommate was a very nice guy with some problems he tried to solve by going to Alaska. It sounds like it worked."

"It has," Annie said. "He's doing very well and has the friendship and respect of the whole town."

"And you? Does he have your friendship and respect as well?" Emmy asked gently.

"You did say 'lived with.'" Terry added.

Annie sipped her tea, considering how to and if she wanted to answer. Finally, she decided, "Can I take you and your husband out to dinner tonight? You too, Terry."

Before Emmy could answer Terry announced that tonight was his poetry class, and he was scheduled to read. He couldn't miss it.

"How about you, Emmy?" Annie asked.

"I'm sure Dave will say okay. He usually cooks and I know he would like a break. I'll call him and let him know. What time?"

Six o'clock was scheduled. Annie and Terry finished their tea and left. The night would hold several surprises.

Meanwhile things were less than ducky down at the moving company. Among the first things I learned about my new job was that the "salary" I was promised was actually a "draw" against my commissions. In plain talk I got a percentage of what moves I booked, period. Uncle Nick's partner, Mike, explained that I would have a ninety-day grace period on my draw and that was it. Then I discovered that my training would consist of riding around with another moving salesman while he made sales calls. He wasn't thrilled to have me along; I wasn't thrilled to be along. I saw very little of Uncle Nick. He spent most of his time out of the office, squiring corporate clients around golf courses, cocktail lounges and strip clubs.

"Mainly we get leads off real estate listings and 'For Sale' signs." Lou Hackett explained. Lou had been given the task of training me by Uncle Nick. He was making the best of it, as was I, at least at first.

After obtaining "the leads" Lou and I would make an unannounced appearance at the residential property to offer a free estimate on any moving expenses. Often, the residents had already endured several prior free offers from competing moving firms such as Mayflower, United Van Lines, Global Van Lines, North American Van lines and a host of others. I also learned that all moving expenses were entirely regulated by the Interstate Commerce Commission. Rates and expenses were mandated by the overall weight of the transported household goods and the mileage involved in the move. Local labor aside, American Red Ball (me and Lou), charged the same as Mayflower, United and all of the above. Sales depended upon timeliness, wishful promises, false assurances and schmoozing. I hated schmoozing, timeliness was pure luck, wishful promises and false assurances were industry standards.

"No offense to you, Lou, but this sucks." Lou and I were driving away from yet another, "Sorry we have already booked a mover," house call and I was getting fed up, fast.

"It's a numbers game, Dave. You just have to have patience," Lou explained. Lou was maybe ten or fifteen years older than me, paunchy, losing his hair and working on a third chin. He wore cheap Sears & Roebuck grey suits with a gravy-stained tie and brown shoes. His interests were network game shows, cocker spaniels and cheap scotch. This was not going to be my future; this was not even going to be my present for very long.

"This isn't what we talked about, Nick."

"What'dya' mean? I said I'd train ya, I'm trainin' ya."

"Training me for what, Nick? I already have a cheap suit."

"Ya wanna' learn the business, you start sellin' moves. I started out on the trucks, loading the trucks."

And I realized the guy had a point, not my point perhaps, but a point, nevertheless.

"You're right, Nick. I apologize for my attitude, but I'll let you know when I've had enough of 'sellin moves.'"

"No, I'll let ya know when you've had enough of sellin' moves. Ya' wanna' learn, you learn my way."

And that's the way it was down at the moving company.

"Tell me again about who's taking us to dinner tonight?" I asked as I changed out of my moving salesman clothes and attitude.

"Her name is Annie DeShay, and she owns these apartments and the rest of it I want to be a surprise."

Emmy had that smile, the good smile, so surprise it would be.

"Where?" I asked.

"Chart House, Dana Point Harbor. Six o'clock."

"Okay."

Annie was seated by the ceiling length windows overlooking the harbor. Pretty girl, nicely dressed, same smile as Emmy. Introductions were made, wine was ordered and then I heard the whole story. LT safe in Alaska, a game warden, town constable, good guy in a good place. I was happy for him.

"I thought after dinner we could give him a call," Annie suggested.

A wonderful idea. So was dinner.

"Lieutenant Robert Baker, I presume?" I was going all mystery voice on our long-distance phone call from Annie's luxury suite at the harbor.

"Former Lieutenant," he answered, tentatively, cautiously.

"It's Dave Ferrier, amigo," I chirped, not wanting to overplay the game.

"Dave!??? How did you find me? How did you get this number? I'm happy to hear from you! What the hell?"

Without answering I handed the phone to Annie. "I gave him the number. I found them, long story for later, here's Dave back. Em, let's you and I go to the cocktail lounge and trade stories about these two while they tell lies about us. We'll talk later, LT," she shouted as she and Emmy left the suite.

"Dave, I'm a little confused," LT said, sounding much more than a little confused.

"That's a big improvement over the last time I saw you," I answered as we began the long and pleasant process of catching up.

LT related the journey to and into Alaska. He talked about the late Colonel Jake Hackleberry, and his reconciliation with his father. I told the Border Patrol tale, the getting married and moving to California tale. He left out his death march to Homer. I left out the tragic birth of Dick Gerson's daughter.

"So, you've got a badge and a gun?" I asked.

"Mostly I've got a canoe and a backpack. Constable's a part time thing here in Homer. What I really enjoy is keeping the wilderness the way it should be."

"What's the deal with Annie?" I finally got around to asking.

"I wish I knew. Apparently, she's pretty wealthy. Her father left her a lot of money which came with a lot of responsibility. She's trying to work it out. I'm trying not to miss her too much."

"She sounds pretty fond of you."

"And I of her," he speculated, "wish me luck with that."

"Always, amigo. Can you take down my home phone number? Let's keep in touch."

LT jotted down the number, I took his and we ended the call. I felt good knowing my friend had done well, is doing well. Now I was on my way to the cocktail lounge to see how I was doing.

"Annie's going to give me a job!" Emmy announced as I seated myself at their table.

"A job?" I asked ordering a draft beer.
Emmy had been looking for work since our move. She was no longer interested in teaching and restaurant hosting paid

pennies, tied up our evenings, and there were the doctors, lawyers and Indian chiefs to fend off.

"I need an assistant, an office manager or whatever it's called. My father's lawyer insists I open an Orange County office of some kind because we own several properties here. I need someone to take calls, relay messages, handle problems. Someone that isn't me, someone I like and feel I can trust. Emmy checks all the boxes," Annie declared.

"That's not even the best part," Emmy added. "I don't really need an office, office, just a phone and an answering machine."

Annie added, "If I put a separate phone line in your apartment, Emmy handles the calls, and I pick up your rent."

"And…" Emmy smiled.

"And $800 a month," Annie replied.

Wow! This was turning into a five-star evening. Great dinner, new friend found, old friend located, our monthly income doubled, and the draft beer was nice and cold.

"So, what did our Alaskan friend have to say?" Annie asked.

"I don't think I'm talking out of turn to tell you he misses you a lot," which got a more than satisfied smile out of Annie, "and he also says the hoary marmots miss you, whatever the hell they are."

"Ah yes, the hoary marmots, listen you two I bet you have a lot to talk about and I am going to give our Alaskan friend a call. Don't worry about the bar tab, it's on my room. Just leave a nice tip. I'll call you in the morning."

Annie took her leave. Emmy looked at me, I looked at Emmy. We were both winning the smiling contest.

"What do you think?" Emmy asked while feeling delighted, as I was.

"I think I'll have another beer."

Some nights are better than others. This one was much better.

"'Infractions' was a mistake," Cindy admitted while she picked at her Ceasar salad. Peter was wise enough not to agree as he nibbled his cheeseburger. "Seemingly trivializing the offense can alienate the Court," Cindy continued, Peter nibbled.

"Cin, that case was a dead bang loser. Third DUI, property damage, stolen car and he swung at a cop. Where's the upside?" Peter suggested, quietly.

"At least the judge disallowed the auto theft, thanks for not objecting," Cindy said.

"I didn't object because I would have had to put Miss Tanguay on the stand and she's a mess. Cin, it's hard being a cop in Lowell. Everybody knows everybody. Every time someone gets arrested he, or she, is someone's son or daughter, best friend or cousin, whatever. The old boy system kicks in. Timmy burned all those bridges. There are two things you don't do in Lowell, bad mouth the Kennedy clan, Jack, Bobby, even Teddy, and you don't take a swing at a cop."

"They beat the shit out of him. Three weeks in the hospital."

"Swinging at a cop in Lowell, that's about low average." Peter put down his cheseburger.

"Cin, you did a good job but the deck was stacked. My asshole boss thought it would be funny to put us up against each other in Court. It wasn't funny and it won't happen again. I'll recuse myself."

"Like hell you will. I want a rematch."

"Cin, I want to be your partner, not your opponent."

Cindy put down her salad fork, remembering why she fell in love with Peter Rayburn. And the music played somewhere…

Just an old fashioned love song,

Playing on the radio,

And wrapped around the music

Is the sound of someone saying

That they'll never go.

You swear you've heard it, before,
As it, slowly rambles on.
No need in bringing 'em back
Cause they've never really gone.

Just, an old fashioned love song,
One I'm sure they wrote for you and
me,

Just, an old fashioned love song,
Coming sown in three part, harmony *

Lyrical Aspirations:
Just an Old Fashioned Love Song , Paul Williams

Chapter Fourteen

Reasons

"I'm not asking you Nick, I'm telling you. Emmy and I are going back to Lowell for a friend's wedding. If you don't want to pay me while I'm gone, don't. If you want to fire me, go ahead, but we are going."

"You've been here, what? A coupla' weeks and you're gonna' take a vacation?" Nick was growling, as usual.

"I've been here two months, Nick. I've been schlepping around with Lou Hackett getting doors slammed in my face. This is not what we discussed."

"Ya' gotta' learn the business."

"What I'm learning is the business sucks. My Dad told me once that finding out what I didn't want to do was as important as finding what I really wanted to do. I'm getting tired of finding out what I don't want to do."

"Relax will ya', if you gotta go to this wedding okay. Just make it up when you get back."

"I'll try Nick, that's the best I can do right now."

"When ya' goin'?"

"Tuesday morning, the wedding's on Saturday. We'll be back late Monday."

"Mike ain't gonna' be happy."

"Making Mike happy is not my job."

"Making me happy is your job and you ain't doin' it."

"Just another thing we have in common Nick."

I could feel my time at American Red Ball movers getting shorter.

"Non, Thanh has her final exams and I must stay for the Gallerie Ete Premiere." Gianna was insistent and correct. "You must go to this wedding alone, for now. One day we all go "pour le grand tour" of your Etats-Unis. Your David must have me meet this John Wayne."

"Your David" rang a hollow bell in Margaret Mary's stomach. Not Her's anymore. There was Emmy, there was Gianna. There was heartache.

Margaret Mary set her course to Lowell for Peter's wedding with a return stop in Dublin for the love of her family. Neither would go as planned or as hoped for.

As her plane descended on final approach to Boston's Logan airport Margaret Mary looked out the window at the familiar skyline of the city. The Prudential Tower dominated, the Harbor and wharfs seemed full of activity, the traffic appeared endless. The city, once practically the end of her universe, felt foreign and faint. This was hardly a homecoming, barely a reunion, more of an obligation to her past which despite the gaiety of the wedding loomed as an uncertain reminiscence of memories from long, long ago.

Peter and his about to be bride were waiting for her in the terminal. Happy hellos were exchanged, introductions were made, friendships were renewed and established. Peter was not wearing a beret, Margaret Mary was, as well as a cape, shamrock green and very stylish. "A cape," Peter thought, "why didn't I ever think of a cape?"

"Thank you so much for coming," Cindy said as they drove north from Boston to Lowell.

"I couldn't miss seeing Peter get married," Margaret Mary replied, "and I couldn't wait to meet the person he chose to marry."

"Truth be told," Cindy replied, "I chose him, but that's a story for when we're alone."

Peter said nothing, eyes straight ahead diligently driving.

"Is David here yet?" Margaret Mary inquired.

"He's coming in tomorrow," Peter answered, "with, you know, his wife."

"I do know his wife," Margaret Mary replied, "I'm happy for him," She sort of lied, which resulted in a heavy silence in the automobile chatter.

Margaret Mary watched the once familiar streets of Lowell glide by as Peter drove to her hotel. Childhood days and childhood dreams flashed past the window only to be interrupted by an empty lot that once was Paradise Donuts, peeling paint and sagging eaves on the Moody School, where the tough guys (and girls) used to go, large brown spots on the once emerald, green baseball field at Shedd park and mounds of litter clogging the curbsides which blighted her memories. The old hometown looked shabby around the edges. Time does not pass gently.

"You must be exhausted from your trip; would you like to get something to eat or go right to your hotel?" Cindy asked.

"I'm too tired to eat; the hotel will be fine and thank you again so much for coming to get me."

Which got a heartfelt "You're welcome" from both Peter and Cindy.

Peter and Cindy dropped Margaret Mary at her hotel but failed to notice she was fighting tears as she said goodbye. Alone in her room, realizing how far from her childhood she had journeyed, how alone in her former hometown she was, she sat on the edge of the bed in her solitary hotel room and cried until she fell asleep.

"LT, it's for you, it's Annie," Bill Lucier, the Legion Hall bartender shouted across the crowded room as he waved the phone receiver.

"Why do you call me at the bar?" LT asked cradling the phone and his coffee against the hubbub of the room.

"Because I know where you are and exactly what you're doing when you are at the Legion Hall. How do I know what's going on up at that house of yours when I'm not there?" Annie teased.

"What's going on at the house when you are not there is too lonely to talk about," LT answered, Annie melted.

"I miss you, a lot," She admitted.

"Me too, when are you coming back? Are you coming back? How long are you coming back for?" LT raced through the questions, longing for the answers.

"Of course I'm coming back, we live there, I've got a job there, and I love you there," Annie answered. LT's head swam, sweet relief smothered lingering sadness. "I've about got things wrapped up here. If I have to go to one more meeting where everybody calls me 'Miss DeShay' every ten seconds I'm going to scream."

LT gave a short laugh, "There are some new folks moved here since you left. I can't get them to stop calling me 'Officer Baker.'"

"Another week, maybe," Annie answered, "Dave's wife Emmy is a gem. She's going to handle my Orange County headaches, I've got lawyers to handle LA, and I'm going to concentrate on handling you."

"Do that soon, will you?" LT pleaded.

"One week, I promise. I'll be there with bells on."

"Bells?" LT asked.

"Just bells," Annie promised,

LT truly, deeply, hoped she would.

Ring-a-ding ding.

'Things are not going well with your Uncle Nick," I admitted while Emmy and I flew east on Delta Flight 308 to Logan Airport in Boston.

"I know," Emmy said, taking my hand in hers. "What are we going to do?"

I loved that she said "we." The whole togetherness business was still new to me. Up till now the only one affected by my choices and behavior was myself, which gave me a lot of latitude regarding personal freedom and personal stupidity. Now there was "we" and I had to grow up another notch and consider that.

Our trip from Laguna Niguel to LAX had been a nightmare. Sixty miles of bumper to bumper traffic on the 405 freeway, inching along Century Boulevard to long term, remote parking and a lumbering, crawling airport bus to a crowded, understaffed, chaotic terminal. Welcome to the real Los Angeles. The one saving grace so far was our decision to fly First Class. The cramped, noisy, soulless seating of our initial coach trip helped us resolve not to repeat that experience, damn the cost.

"I'm not sure, Em. I know I can find another job, it's the whole family thing I'm concerned about."

"Nick told Joan he doesn't think you're ambitous enough," Em said, pissing me off.

"What I'm not is intimidated enough, Em. Nick likes to bark at people, he's a bully at work and he's tried that shit on me too. It isn't going to work."

Of that I was sure, we or no we. Emmy squeezed my hand and said, "Good."

I told you she was a keeper.

Then the stewardess offered us champagne. Things were looking up.

When we landed at Logan airport my Mom and Dad were waiting for us. Em's mother, Mary, was there as well and there were huge smiles and hugs all around. We gathered luggage and piled into my Dad's station wagon for the ride up to Lowell.

"Are you guys hungry?" my Dad asked.

"Starving!" Emmy and I said in chorus.

Which resulted in a stop at Kitty's Restaurant and Lounge in North Redding where I ate enough fried clams, french fries and onion rings to feed the whole table while the others enjoyed Kitty's justifiably famous pizza. Table conversation was friendly and famished. I had already explained to my Mom and Dad that Emmy and I were going to stay at Mary's house while in town. Emmy was considerably homesick and I wanted her to spend as much time with her family as possible while we were here. Mom and Dad understood. Glenmere Street would be a visit, not a lodging for the next week or so. Strange feeling.

Emmy and I thirsted after the local news and learned that generally all was well. My brother John had moved to Florida with a bunch of friends, Bob was still at home but looking for an apartment with his girlfriend. Sadly, we were told that Teddy had moved to Lawrence, abandoning his family after losing his job with the police department. He had also abandoned Alcoholics Annonymous and was said to be drinking heavily and getting worse. I would look into this later, Teddy was my buddy. Margaret Mary was in town and had called my Mom and Dad earlier in the day. She couldn't wait to see me and meet Emmy. That was going to be an interesting get together.

Later that evening as Emmy and I settled into her childhood, 'little too girly for me' bedroom, I reflected on the day's events. My job situation with American Red Ball was looking precarious, fried is the only way to eat clams, the old home town looked very old, and tomorrow I would introduce my wife to the girl I always thought I would marry. Thankfully, exhuastion descended before I could dwell too long on that circumstance.

Then came the dawn.

Em and I were picking up Margaret Mary for breakfast. We had spoken, at length, about my deep friendship and relationship with Margaret Mary over the many years. Em was understanding and considerate, as she always had been. I recounted our history from puppy love to teenage romance, and after my trip to Paris, a deep and abiding friendship I wanted very much to sustain. Em nodded and smiled and took my hand as we drove along. I wondered if I could be as understanding should she want to maintian a friendship with her high school romance and once upon a time fiance, who was, currently serving a lengthy term in Walpole State prison for a drunk driving manslaughter.

Me? Nah, no chance. I wasn't that nice a guy, but I was very grateful that Em was that nice a person.

When we arrived at the hotel Margaret Mary looked better than I had ever seen her. Heartstopping. She was dressed in what I can only describe as ultra-Parisian, very continental, very fashionable. An elegant gray skirt reached her ankles and very fashionable black boots peeked out from beneath. Her blouse was a pearly white with a crushed velvet jacket of deep blue over it. I noticed she was also wearing a silver and turqouise bracelet straight out of El Paso, Texas. The most beautiful thing about her however was her smile, I missed it so much.

"Em, this is my treasured, truest, best, best friend, Margaret Mary Sullivan." Em smiled, Margaret Mary smiled, I froze. We all smiled at each other. Seconds passed, slowly. Ice formed.

"David, if you do not give your truest and best friend a hug very soon I am going to smack you," Em declared. The ice shattered. Margaret Mary and I hugged, hard. My heart pounded, her eyes shimmered, we seperated, slowly.

"And I would like a hug as well," Em added. So they did.

"I am so happy to meet you," Em said, "Dave has told me so much about you."

"And I, you," Margaret Mary replied. "We have so much to talk about, I hope we can be friends."

"We shall be," Em answered, "I promise."

Now that's a keeper.

Over breakfast Margaret Mary told us about her and Gianna's adoption of Thanh. There were pictures. There were congratultions. There were invitations. Em and I spoke of California, the Good, the Bad, and the Ugly. Mostly the Good though.

"I want you two to come visit me in Paris. We have lots of room and I would love to show you my city." Most of this was directed to Em, of course. I had seen Margaret Mary's city, I knew about the love and already had the visit. Em looked at me, smiling. I could only nod, knowingly.

I clearly recall as I sat there watching my wife converse with my not so secret love, how much times had changed, even if I had not. My feelings for Margaret Mary did hinder my feelings for Emmy and I now realized those feelings had to subside, or at least should diminish. Margaret Mary had her life in Paris, Em and I were struggling to make a life in California and never, as Samuel Clemens predicted, "the twain shall meet." Part of me said goodbye to part of Margaret Mary. Perhaps that is what growing up is all about.

The Immaculate Conception church was ablaze with tall and small candles, colorful white and red roses lined the aisles, incense burned abundantly and stained glass windows sparkled as Peter and Cindy walked down the church's center aisle while the thunderous pipe organ played the wedding march. Peter's parents beamed with pride, Cindy's mother wept with joy, the assembled congregation beamed with happiness. Father Scanlon officiated, Peter glowed, Cindy behaved, the deal was done.

Lawyers in love.

Peter and Cindy's wedding reception was a gala and a goodbye. My old crowd was breaking up, growing up and growing far apart as the years passed. Margaret Mary would return to Paris, via Dublin, the very next day, two days earlier than she planned. Loneliness and her newly acknowledged Lowell blues were the persuaders. Peter and Cindy were off to Bermuda, honeymooners that they were. Teddy was gone and living in Lawrence, a town some twenty miles and twenty heartaches away. Beth said he was lost in alcohol and despair. She had not heard from him in over six months. I tried to find him twice. He avoided me both times. Actions speak louder than words. I would try again. Teddy is my buddy.

There was, however, one wedding reception moment that stood out above all the others. The many tiered white cake was cut and shared, a bright red garter was tossed to the crowd, toasts and tributes were hoisted and guzzled, the bride and groom solo danced magically to Bobby Darin's bouncy rendition of "Just in Time" and then it happened, if not pre-planned, certainly inevitable. Cindy, in her wedding white with her wicked smile joined Margaret Mary in her elegant silver gown and Emmy, resplendent as ever in hushed violet as they joined hands on the empty dance floor, signaled to the band and danced to the slowest, sexiest, sultriest rendition of the Hokey-Pokey ever seen at Vesper, or any other country club. Peter blushed, I gaped, Father Scanlon applauded, and the children silently watched in wonder.

There were one or two more surprises before Emmy and I were to return to California. First and foremost was that Emmy didn't want to leave. She asked, even pleaded, for us to stay another few days. She missed her mother and sister a lot. She missed Lowell, the barking Greeks, her local friends, her community, creased edges and all. Just a few more days she asked. So we did.

Uncle Nick hit the roof when I called him. "If you ain't back on Monday, you don't need to come back at all!" He barked.

I chose at all, and Emmy. We stayed four more days and I was out of a job.

My Dad told me he was retiring in six months and that he and my Mom were going to sell our Glenmere Street home and move to Florida, the Valhalla of New England retirees. They made a visit to where my brother John, was staying with his friends and really liked the area. Melbourne, Florida it was. In six months. Life changes rapidly.

I made a third and final trip to Lawrence to look for Teddy and found him working as a security guard at a Raytheon plant. He looked terrible. Fat, sloppy and angry. Angry at me for finding him, angry at Raytheon for sticking him in a guard shack, angry at the world and everything in it, especially his disabled, struggling daughter whom he had not seen for six months.

"Buncha' shit," he growled when I ran him down. "And you shouldna' come here either," he added, "I don''t wanna' talk to you."

And he wouldn't, so I left, leaving my former best buddy in a pit of self pity and despair.

The next morning Emmy and I flew back to California. And a song whispered…

It never rains in Southern California,
Seems I've often heard that kind of
talk before,

It never rains in Southern California,
But girl, don't they warn ya'
It pours, man, it pours. *

Lyrical Aspirations:
It Never Rains In Southern California, Albert Hammond

Chapter Fifteen

Reckonings

Uncle Nick fired me when Emmy and I got back to California. Or I quit, it was kind of a tie. I think I quit; he thinks he fired me. Either way I was out of a job, with pleasure. Em and I had about three thousand dollars in savings; Annie DeShay was picking up our rent at Sea View Apartments so there was enough slack in the line for me to look around for a better next job. When I found it, things really started to go off the tracks, it paid me way too much money.

The Brown & Williamson Tobacco company makes and distributes Kool, Raleigh, Viceroy, Bel Air and Barclay Cigarettes. On the tobacco trade importance tree, they were a healthy third behind the Marlboro and Winston conglomerates, but all the cigarette companies were doing a booming business in the late seventies, early eighties. Smoking was cool, suave, sophisticated and horribly addicting, but nobody paid much attention to that last part. Doctors, athletes, movie stars, housewives and politicians all smoked copiously, safe in the assurance that cigarettes were harmless, actually good for you.

I started smoking in high school. Smoking was practically a required course at Lowell High when I was there. I kept it up through the Army, college and American Red Ball movers. Then Brown & Williamson offered me a job, a high paying, benefit laden, management job, with an expense account, a company car and free cigarettes. I accepted, life was good, for a while.

I was hired to manage the Orange County, California retail distribution of our products. I had six minions who worked for me running around setting up displays and rotating product. Orange County is a sprawling, prosperous Caucasian ghetto of upscale tract housing, shopping centers, liquor stores, tennis courts and golf courses. Rampant Consumerism at its very best. Prime cigarette selling country. I did well as a regional manager type. I assembled a team of six conscientious, hardworking people I did not need to babysit or cajole. They did their job, I did mine. All was well.

Meanwhile Emmy and I were patronizing better restaurants much more often. I learned my way around a wine list. We ordered appetizers before our meals and dined overlooking the Pacific Ocean every Friday night. Six months after I started with Brown & Williamson, Emmy and I purchased our first home, a nice condominium in San Juan Capistrano. Emmy moved the Annie DeShay telephone from Sea View Apartments to our new home. Annie increased Em's salary by four hundred bucks a month. "And the money just kept on rollin' in."

And the bad habits started. Em got a new car. I got a new stereo, then a newer one. The TV got larger, the furniture got plusher, we discovered Las Vegas weekends "And the money just kept on rollin' out."

The more we made, the more we spent, just like everyone else we knew. There was no way this was going to end well.

"I don't know, Annie, marriage is kind of a big step, you know?" LT gulped as he and Annie sat on the brand new front porch of what had once been Lieutenant Colonel Hackleberry's modest cottage. LT's game warden salary and Annie's "Big Bucks" had resulted in several cottage upgrades, major, minor and luxurious. Annie and LT had been living together for almost a year, Annie running her inheritance from afar, LT keeping the streams and woodlands clean and clear while town constabling on the side.

"In or out," Annie declared, "you've passed the audition and I assume I have as well. Time for the next step."

Next steps were coming easier for LT as of late. He had come a long way from marching down the Seward Highway looking for a place to freeze to death to relaxing on his front porch with a woman he loved. They were even talking about having a baby. Next steps indeed.

"I love you Annie and I want nothing more than to be your husband, but what in the world do you see in me?" LT wasn't fooling, he couldn't imagine what Annie saw in him any more than he could ever imagine leaving Homer or Annie wanting to stay there.

"Are you looking for compliments big guy?" Annie replied, "You're honest and you work hard and you love your job and I know you love me. Is that enough?"

More than enough, LT knew. "But what about here? In Homer? You have mentioned the big, wide world to me a time or two."

"I've kept the home in Santa Barbara, I would like us to spend some time there, particularly in the winter when this place is hell in an icebox. We can work on that, we can work on everything if you're as willing as I am."

LT was willing, he was more than willing. He was United States Marine Corps more than willing. A wedding date was proposed. Homer, Alaska was going to have a gala wedding celebration in the fall.

Margaret Mary had a stopover in Ireland on her way home from Peter and Cindy's wedding. She found Sean and Rose to be distressed, heartbroken over what was happening in their beloved country. In the past year over four hundred British soldiers and Irish civilians had been killed as Protestants and Catholics, Separatists and Loyalists, men, women and children died as "The Troubles" raged on. The hatred, the fear, the animosity in the country was so thick you could cut it with a knife. No Yeats, no Wilde, no James Joyce or Eavan Boland could salve the wounds that bled the country.

"But why, Da?" Margaret Mary pleaded. "Why so much hate?"

"The Catholics hate the Brits, the Protestants hate the Catholics, they both hate those who do not hate enough, tears of rage overwhelm our Ireland," Sean whispered, the sound of sadness softening his voice.

"We live in wretched times, love," Rose added, "wretched times I see no end to."

"Then you must come and live in my beautiful Paris! It is safe there, we can be together there," Margaret Mary pleaded.

"My heart is here, daughter, in Ireland. Wherever I would travel I would be here," Sean answered.

"And I as well," Rose said, each with the souls of the bleeding Irish.

And so went their time together. During her visit pubs were bombed, British soldiers were kidnapped and killed, buildings burned and politicians argued, all to no avail. After three short days Margaret Mary was once again ready to return to her home in Paris.

"Won't you at least come and stay for a visit?" She pleaded.

"I cannot child. I have my courses at the University, your aunt has her bakery. The worst of the worst is in the north. Belfast suffers most of all. We are safe here, for now at least, the troubles are in the North."

"The troubles are in all of Ireland," Rose reminded.

"Perhaps for the holidays then," Sean promised. "Christmas in Paris, all of us together."

"Christmas then," Margaret Mary agreed, "but you must call, every day, more even. I am afraid for you."

"We will stay safe, daughter. And call we will, if not every day, enough for you to know we are alright." Sean hugged his daughter hard, Rose wiped away a tear, and Margaret Mary boarded her plane for the two hour flight to Paris.

Man plans, God laughs.

"Wear the wig!" Eddie reminded, "They got cameras in that place too." Eddie was talking to his new paramour, Carmen Bonita-Sanchez, who was about to set off to place a number of hefty wagers with Eddie's money on Sunday's National Football League action at several off-strip betting parlors.

Carmen was a cocktail waitress at Eddie's casino of employment, big smile, big chest, big ambitions. She wanted to be a movie star, all she lacked was talent and money and connections. She needed acting lessons, wardrobe, a professional portfolio of steamy photographs, and a trip to Hollywood. Her needs list required more money than a cocktail waitress pulled down. Over the course of several overnight encounters she had come to believe Eddie had a knack for making extra money and the connections she needed. Hence the wig.

Las Vegas casinos discouraged, forbade would be a better word, their employess to gamble on their working premises. They had no objection to these folks trying to get closer to twenty-one at other casinos, or pulling the handles of the competition's one armed bandits, but sports betting, on or off premises, was frowned upon, and scrutinized. Casino personnel had access to betting information unknown to the general public. A sharp guy watching the point spreads and the betting line could predict a winner with a lot more accuracy than some Joe from the street. Sports betting pros were tolerated, until they became too successful. Then they were blacklisted. Sports betting casino employees could get fired, then blacklisted, if they were lucky. This information did not phase Eddie, or Carmen.

"The Goddamn thing itches my head!" Carmen whined.

"Itching ain't the worst thing that could happen to your head they catch us betting," Eddie reminded.

It had taken Eddie about six months to figure out what corners he could cut in his new job. He didn't steal, never took bribes and got along with his bosses and the patrons. He kept his nose clean while noticing how uncannily accurate the point spreads on professional football games were, especially at the end of the week when the big money was all laid down. Adjustments in the betting line were made, just before games were played. The casinos did very well. Eddie learned to get in late, follow the casino's betting pool and keep a low profile.

Carmen made the off-Strip betting parlor rounds, big wigs, bimbo glasses, lots of chest, shiny pants. She spread the bets out, a couple thousand at each venue. She did not collect the winnings. Eddie had another partner, a Chinese cab driver named Tommy Tang. He wore sharkskin suits, dark glasses and aligator shoes. They divvied up, fifty for Eddie, twenty five each for Carmen and Tommy. What could go wrong?

In the Fall, Emmy and I flew into Fairbanks, Alaska on a brisk autumn afternoon in September of 1978. Annie DeShay had insisted on making the trip a company excursion given Emmy's role as Orange County manager of DeShay Enterprises. Plane tickets, hotels, meals and sled dogs, if necessary, were all on the company plan. A wedding was in the offing.

I couldn't wait to see LT. We had stayed in touch by phone over the last year, but no plans had worked out for a face to face. Until now.

LT and Annie were waiting for us at the airport. LT was in his Game Warden green uniform, sort of Border Patrol military without the swagger, or the shotgun. Annie beamed, I smiled, Emmy outdressed us all.

"Too, too long, my brother," LT proclaimed as he wrapped me in a bear hug.

"Absolutely," I countered, glad in my heart to see my old friend again. Meanwhile Annie and Em hugged as well, introductions were made, LT had never met Em, and the trip from the airport began.

The two hundred and twenty something mile trip from Fairbanks to Homer took us between the Chugach Mountains and Cook Inlet, past waterfalls, scenic outlooks and vistas more beautiful than I had ever seen. Snow capped the surrounding mountain peaks year round, the Inlet's ocean was the deepest blue, the forests the greenest green, the sky clear and clean and beautiful. A stark contrast to Los Angeles and Orange County's dingy brown air and hazy San Bernadino mountains, barely visible most days due to the urban smog. The trip to Homer took six hours with turnouts, rest areas, lunch and overlooks.

When we finally arrived Em and I were exhuasted. The town looked quaint, comfortable, and welcoming. Annie had personally arranged for the local motel/lodge to remain open and we were shown to our room, very hunting lodge-ish, lots of fireplace and pine logs and stuffed dead animals. We unpacked, LT and Annie said they would pick us up for dinner. A nap was in order then let the festivities begin.

"I never thought I'd see this thing again," LT said as I handed him his 1911 Colt 45 automatic, beautifully mounted and framed in a lacquered shadow box with plaque and USMC Birdie on the Ball emblem as a pre-wedding, hello again gift. The plaque read, "You don't hurt 'em if you don't hit 'em" Chesty Puller, USMC. The quote was my idea, the shadow box was Emmy's.

LT left the pistol behind with me when he departed Amherst four years ago. That and a chest full of medals he earned in Vietnam. Emmy had the medals arranged in the shadow box as well. LT looked surprised - stunned and proud as he showed Annie a bit of his past he had barely spoken of before. He tried to say thank you and choked up. I knew all about that damned lump in the throat thing. I was happy for my friend.

Dinner was the most delicious baked halibut I had ever tasted. LT's Mom, having flown in from Florida two days earlier, joined us for the meal. She beamed with pride at her son, clung to Annie like she was her own daughter and delighted us with tales of young Bobby Baker, pre-Marine Corps adolescent and scalawag.

Annie was bereft of family but was expecting a corporate attendant or two to arrive for the wedding. Dinner however , was ours alone and delightful. An Alaskan State Trooper named Luke Drayber dropped by after the meal. He was LT's best man for the ceremony. The only other guests invited were the entire population of Homer, and a few surrounding campsites. As we ate in the local VFW hall the townspeople of Homer came by our table, offering welcome to Em and I, congratulations to LT and Annie and leaving behind a sense of commumnity and fraternity I had not experienced in a long, long time. I needed more of that.

I cannot remember ever sleeping deeper, sounder or more comfortably than that first night in Homer. Em and I sank beneath handmade quilts with our heads atop goose down pillows, before a smoldering fireplace in absolute, pine log crackling stillness. Before plunging off to sleep I reviewed a very good day. Good friends, good food, clean air, a warm bed and a loving wife. I needed less of Orange County sales schmoozing and corporate clammoring. I craved the respect and fellowship directed at LT and Annie by their community. And a tiny seed of unrest was rekindled.

I was becoming very good at being a cigarette salesman, lots of money, lots of perks. So what? I was getting those "old kosmic blues" again, feeling prosperous, but unfulfilled, even during the best of times, like right now. Changes were stirring. Em whispered goodnight, I answered very, very good night and made myself a promise to reexamine my priorities, a promise I was determined to keep.

The next day LT and Annie took Em and I for a stroll along the colorfully named "Homer Spit" which turned out to be an elongated strip of land jutting out into the Kachemak Bay lined with shops, art galleries, and small cafes. We walked, we talked. Em and Annie hung back talking wedding things and woman's secrets. LT and I marched ahead.

"So you like being a cigarette salesman?" LT asked, just a hint of skepticism in his voice.

"Pays well," I offered, "they treat me very well."

LT grunted and changed the subject. "How's your buddy Ted? He doin' alright?"

So I laid out the entire sad tale. LT was aware of the Agent Orange lawsuit, as were many of Alaska's expatriate Vietnam veterans. Many had come here to escape their troubles, bad memories and experiences. Old troubles follow, new geography seldom helps.

"You ever hear from any of the guys from UMass? The vets?" LT asked.

I hadn't, hadn't tried to reach out to them either. The river flows fast. I thought of them occassionally, Roomie Ron, Dick Greyson, Lucius, even Rootin' Tootin', but they were fading, just like Woody and Harry and Don and all the guys from Nam. I didn't like looking back, partly because I didn't like where I was looking back from.

"I'm drifting, LT," I began, saying out loud what had been bothering me for weeks, months. "Two years in Nam, lots of near misses, too much body count and here I am selling cigarettes and playing country club tennis."

"The American Dream?" LT answered, skeptically.

"The only American Dream I've ever had was that I wouldn't get my ass shot off in Nam," I answered.

"Congratulations, you win the big prize, it's called Survivor Guilt."

"Lucky me, I guess."

"Nothing guilty about surviving, Dave. Random chance, pure luck, reasonable caution, maybe, but guilt? About what?"

"Being there, being here, trying to make it count I guess."

"Cigarette salesman isn't doing that for you?"

"Not hardly."

"Then you better figure out what does."

He was right, of course. Which meant I was wrong, for now.

Thanh raced across the airport terminal the moment she spotted Margaret Mary exiting the plane. She rushed to her, threw her arms around her legs and was happy, happy. Gianna hurried to catch up, smiling as well.

"Bienvenue a la maison," Gianna said.

"Bienvenue ma mere," echoed Thanh as Margaret Mary's heart melted.

"You look tired, and you look sad," Gianna commented when they returned to their home and took seats on the patio. Margaret Mary answered with a sigh and sipped the wine Gianna had poured for both of them.

"The trip was long, and …sad," She answered.

"And why the sadness?" Gianna asked.

"Lowell, the town I grew up in, looked…tired, run down. The old familiar sites looked old and unfamiliar. David's wife is very beautiful, and he," Margaret Mary hesitated searching for the right word, "he has a 'bedonnant.'"

Gianna could not hold back a laugh. "Pot belly? Your David has a pot belly?"

Margaret Mary tried not to smile, and lost the struggle, but only for a moment. "He looked different, happy, but pretending to be happier than he was."

"Aren't we all like that sometimes?" Gianna offered.

"Not so much as what I saw," Margaret Mary replied sadly.

"And your Pere and Tante, Rose? They are well?"

"They are well, Ireland is not. So much anger, tension eveywhere. I am afraid for them."

"They should come here," Gianna replied immediately, "live with us, It is safe here."

"Their hearts are with Ireland, there they will stay. Dublin is far from Belfast where the biggest troubles go on and on."

Just then Thanh appeared holding a painting she made for Margaret Mary's homecoming. A beautiful sunflower, potted and resting on a window sill, blue sky and green fields beyond.

"For you Mama," Thanh said in her rapidly improving English. This was not the work of a child, but of a very promising young artist.

"She works with our Jean Michael in his studio after school. She is doing well, no?" Gianna smiled.

"Very well," Margarret Mary answered while hugging Thanh.

"You like it, Mama? It can go to the gallery?" Thanh hoped.

"Never, ever," Margaret Mary replied, "this stays with me, my gift, it shall hang here in our home for only our best friends to see."

"One day I shall make a painting for the gallery," Thanh announced.

"One day you will do many things," Margaret Mary answered, "and yes, I believe many of them will hang in our gallery."

And the gloom of her trip lifted as Mararet Mary savored her family and their future.

Among the first things Em and I noticed, grumpily, upon our return to Los Angeles was how brown the sky was, how congested the traffic was and how superficial our lives there had become. I suited up, showed up and resumed my diligent sales and distribution duties for the Brown & Williamson tobacco company. Em caught up with Terry Trent and smoothed the wrinkles in Annie's Orange County enterprises. But the thrill was fading fast. Em and I made renewed efforts to get to know our condominium neighbors but most of them were too busy to socialize and the "hominess" of Homer was nowhere to be found. But for Emmy these circumstances were secondary to her most pressing, unspoken heartache. I was soon to learn just how distressing this was for her.

Change, changes, were once again upon the horizon. Some of them would be for the better, others not so much.

Onward to the music…

So far away
Doesn't anybody stay in one place
anymore?
It would be so fine to see your face at my
door

Doesn't help to know you're just time away
Long ago, I reached for you and there you
stood

Holding you again could only do me good

How I wish I could, but you're so far
away *

Lyrical Aspirations:
So Far Away, Carol King

Chapter Sixteen

Huggles and Struggles

"Have a seat Eddie."

The first thing Eddie noticed after being called into his manager's office at the Golden Grand was the pile of bleach blond hair on the desktop. It looked familiar.

"We got a problem, Eddie. You know what this is?" Eddie's boss, Max Mecham, asked as he dangled the hair ball in front of Eddie.

Eddie knew. "Carmen, right?" He admitted.

"Carmen wrong, Eddie. You know the rules about sports betting?"

Eddie nodded again. Ma's gonna' be pissed, he pondered as Max dropped the wig back onto the desktop.

"How?" was all Eddie could think of to ask.

"Parking lots got cameras too, Eddie. You know that, I know that, Carmen on the other hand did not know that."

Silence filled the room. Eddie stared at the wig. Max stared at Eddie.

"She okay?" Eddie asked.

"She is on a bus to Los Angeles. Took a fistful of your money and one suitcase with her. She told me to tell you goodbye. Your cab driver, Mr. Tang, did the same. He headed west, cab and all."

"Am I fired?" Eddie asked.

Max let the question hang in the air for a moment.

"I like you, Eddie. You're good with the customers, show up on time for all your shifts, no drugs, no alcohol, your tally is always right, but…"

Eddie squirmed in his seat. He knew what "but" meant.

"What do ya' know about college football, Eddie?" Max asked out of the blue.

"I handled the betting cards a few years back. Good money makers."

"They're better than good, Eddie. They're a gold mine. Do you know how many colleges have football teams in this country?"

"Couple hundred, I guess."

"Eight hundred and fifty-eight, Eddie. That's over four hundred games every weekend for twelve weeks, then the playoffs, the Bowl Games, a gold mine I tell ya'."

"Better than the pros?" Eddie asked, anything to keep the conversation going.

"There are 32 teams in the NFL, 16 games a weekend. Televised, scrutinized, analyzed."

"Legit?" Eddie asked.

"I'd never say otherwise," Max replied cryptically, "Lots of eyes on those games. Do you know how much is bet on the NFL every week, and annually, including the Super Bowl?

"Buncha' millions," Eddie answered.

"Billions, Eddie, Billions. Close to a billion alone, just on the Super Bowl. Events like that cannot be left to random chance. It's bad business. You know how often the favorites win on any given Sunday?"

"Sixty, sixty five percent," Eddie answered, "I figured, lot more in the playoffs."

"Ya' know how often it is in the college games?"

Eddie didn't know.

"Me neither," Max answered, "not across the board anyway. Small colleges, good action, plenty of games, nobody's watchin' so much. Lots of wiggle room."

"Max, what's this got to do with me?"

"Bimbos in itchy wigs is no way to run a sporting enterprise Eddy. And you forgot the most important rule of them all, 'Don't shit where you eat.' Let's just say that for now you are on temporary suspension from the Grand, but if you want to put on your travellin' shoes I got a job for ya'."

Ma's gonna' be pissed, Eddie thought as Max explained.

"Dave, do you ever think we could move back to Lowell?" Emmy asked, no pleaded, in an increasingly frequent San Juan Capistrano conversation. Truth was I wasn't happy with our life, Em was miserable and SoCal was turning into Thunderdome. Miles of around the clock stuck traffic, crime in areas of the city more dangerous than Phu Bai, air that got browner every day, and a placid, desperate conformity that ruled life in southern Orange County.

This was year three of the California Dream and it was getting less dreamy each year. In 1976 there were 2,220 murders in the Golden State, 1977 climbed to 2,515 and now, 1978, the figure was 2,611. Violent crimes of all types were also escalating at a similar, disastrous pace. There were large sections of LA one just didn't go into, the divide was not racial, it was economic. Orange County, where Em and I lived, was relatively safe, as it was relatively prosperous. One had to be careful in the poor parts of town however and LA's poor parts of town were getting bigger and bigger as the poor folk began robbing the rich folk.

The saddest part of all this was the realization that the unhappiness we were both feeling with our location was seeping over into our relationship. We were becoming a partnership in misery. Mine was still vocational, what the hell was I doing with my life? Em's was geographical, she missed Lowell and her family and the Greek community she had grown up in. This was her secret sadness, now repeatedly out in the open.Neither problem was going to be solved by my selling cigarettes in Orange County. We tried to compensate.

In a desperate and foolish move to become genuine Southern Californians, Em and I joined the Mission Viejo Country club. Tennis membership only, no golf. Who had time for golf? Now Em was many wonderful things, a beautiful woman, a charming hostess, a fashion expert, and an overall good person, but what she was not, not even close to being, was any sort of athlete. Em didn't like to get sweaty, have her hair messed up, or bounce around chasing a tennis ball, or any kind of ball at all. So she took tennis lessons. Her instructor refunded our money after three lessons. Em not only didn't much care if she actually hit the tennis ball, she had no conception of where it would go after she accidently hit it. Mostly she stood still and tried not to sweat. But she looked good, a couple hundred dollars worth of tennis outfits with matching earrings will do that. After a few weeks of not really knowing, or caring how to keep score, Emmy concentrated on the country club patio lounge, Margaritas, snacks and gossip.

I started climbing the club's "C" tennis ladder. I loved beating the dentists, accountants and real estate agents. What I didn't love was having a beer or two with them after the games. Most of these guys were actively cheating on their wives, cheating on their taxes and, I assumed, cheating at tennis. They quacked about how much money they made, how much money they spent, what a pain in the ass their kids were and what kind of sports car they were going to buy next. The ones with girl friends on the side were pretty open about it, except when the wives were around of course. I not only had nothing in common with these guys, I didn't want to have anything in common with them. So much for the country club life.

"Not too many ways I can make a living in Lowell, Em," I answered, telling half the truth.

"How do you know, you never even really tried?" She answered, telling all the truth.

"Truth is Em, I don't want to live in Lowell, I don't want to live in New England. The whole place seems old to me, tired, worn out, I don't know how to say it properly, but Lowell is my past, I don't really know where I'm headed yet, and yes, it's getting late for me to find out, but Lowell seems backward."

Em's eyes were full of tears. We had just passed a place neither of us really wanted to go, a vast difference in our concept of a future together had been breached. This wasn't good, and the worst was yet to come.

Over the next few months Em made several trips back to Lowell to visit her family, two of them without me. Corporate responsibilities, corporate excuses. Then the bad thing happened. Em's mother, Mary, had a stroke. She was housebound and frail in the aftermath and needed care. Em flew home immediately to help. Two weeks passed, then a month. We spoke every day. I was planning to fly back as soon as I got a break from work, then Em announced, "Dave, I'm going to stay here with my mother, I don't want to come back to California."

I caught the earliest flight I could get back to Lowell.

"Do you want a divorce?" I asked, hoping I didn't already know the answer.

Em shook her head slowly, up and down, not side to side. She was crying. I was stunned. I knew she was unhappy in

California of course, so was I. But I had not thought her unhappiness had gone this far.

"I can't leave my mother," she sobbed, "and I don't want to go back to California."

That was pretty much it then. There was more conversation of course, expressions of regret on both our parts, but our positions remained the same. I didn't know exactly what I was going to do next, but I wasn't moving back to Lowell. I was going back to California. Em was staying in Lowell. We were getting a divorce.

Love hurts.

"I'm really sorry to hear that, Dave," Cindy said as I visited her law office beneath Fudgie's Pool Hall the next day. She was surprised to see me of course, no one knew I was in town except Emmy and her family. Peter was on his way over from the Prosecutor's office. I needed to make a plan.

"Me too," I answered, "but things haven't been going very well for us for a while now. She wants what she wants, so do I."

Cindy was lawyer enough not to philosophize. "What is it you want me to do?"

"Draw up the paperwork, I guess. I'll sell our condo and send Em the money. We ought to get a pretty good piece of change, real estate has gone way up since we moved in. We talked about it and I'll give her the equity as a settlement and get all her stuff shipped back."

"She agreed to that?" Cindy asked.

"She said so, give her a call and make sure. If we need to make any changes let me know. I want to keep it fair."

Which is when Peter breezed in, all smiles, until he sensed the atmosphere.

"What?" He asked. "What's wrong?"

Explanations and diplomacies followed. There was a gloomy lunch where I learned that Peter was leaving the Prosecutor's office and the independent law firm of Rayburn and Rayburn was about to be launched. Peter reported that the Agent Orange lawsuit was moving ahead equitably and that their mentor and friend Horatio Marks was spearheading the settlement and forcing the Veteran's Administration to acknowledge and take responsibilty for the resulting disabilities.

"H is a good man," I said, "Please tell him I said hello and congratulations."

They did. I took a melancholy flight back to Los Angeles, contacted a realtor and made plans to adjust to my renewed bachelorhood.

Throughout the fall and winter seasons La Impression II continued to thrive, becoming a perennial cultural and financial success story. Thanh visited both Dublin and Florence in the company of her very proud adoptive parents. She learned to love the hornpipe in Dublin and the cheesecake in Florence. Sean and Rose were thrilled at meeting their newly embraced niece and Gianna's parents were enchanted by the child. Life, for this very Parisian family, was good and getting even better.

"Yes, to America," Margaret Mary promised, "Perhaps next spring or late summer when the autumn leaves begin to fall." Thanh was thrilled, then asked, "Maybe we can find my father there!" Margaret Mary was unable to look her child in the eye when she answered, "Perhaps, perhaps we will." Which of course, they wouldn't.

"Ivy League Football Eddie, Harvard, Yale, Princeton, Brown, Boolah-boolah, all those Joe College preppy guys. Lots of egghead alumni, proffesors and accountants, prosperous and proud, mostly don't know shit about football except to rah-rah for the home team," Max explained.

"And what does this have to do with me?" Eddie asked cautiously.

"Me, and a few of my asssociates are going to sponsor several homecoming weekend celebrations at these bastions of higher education. Frat house kind of thing, big football celebrations, lots of booze, rich alumni, lots of bets. We need somebody to be at those parties taking the right bets."

"What do you mean, the right bets? These games juiced?" Eddie asked.

"I would never say that," Max replied.

"Why me?" Eddie added.

"You are currently available and you know the ground."

"Look, uh, Max, I'm kinda' still on probation from back in Boston. Might be best I don't get involved in this kind of stuff."

"Eddie, we know all about your probation status back in Boston. More important is your probation status right here with us. What I'm explaining to you is how to make up for your probation status with us."

"Still, you know, maybe I should just drive a hack, keep my nose clean for a while. Thanks for asking me though," Eddie stammered.

"I'm sorry Eddie, you put me in a delicate position. Did I, at any time, give you the impression that I was asking?"

Eddie was going on the road. His mother was going to be pissed.

Southern California has a service for everything. If you've got the money, someone's got the service. I found the one for moving ex-wives belongings back to New England, as well as the one which sells condominiums quick, and in no time I was sitting in a mostly empty bachelor apartment in Newport Beach, California. Alone again, naturally?

It was lonely without Em, sometimes, but honestly, it was liberating as well. My career in cigarette sales took another deep dive in importance and my self evaluation and sense of purpose moved back into the forefront of my ponderings. I still suited up, showed up for work and was good at my job. They paid well and I was stashing the cash. A change, likley to be financially challenging, was coming.

Emmy called often for the first month or so and I looked forward to her calls but my decision not to move back to Lowell was absolutley firm and the calls slowed down. When my divorce became final I became "Mr. Fix-him-up-with a friend" to the tennis club set. This resulted in meeting a lot of bitter, angry single moms who were not going to start barking at my door. A bachelor I was, a swinger I was not.

My apartment gradually filled up with garage sale furniture, I ate a lot of take out food and watched movies, mostly westerns, to the wee hours. My size 32-30 jeans got unmanageably tight and 34-30's were getting snug as well. I was huffing and puffing on the tennis courts. Bachelorhood was not going as anticipated, but the money was good even if the life wasn't.

"Would you consider relocating to Phoenix?"

My boss at Brown & Williamson, Dan Prescott, was offering me a new job, a raise and a way out of Southern California.

"To be a Regional Manager?" I asked.

"Bill Bruton is retiring, we think you are the guy to replace him," Dan answered.

"It's a big move, Dan. Can I have a few days to think about it?"

"Of course, but don't take too long, Bill leaves in a month and we'd like to get you settled in over there before that."
Well, I now had a way out of Southern California if not out of cigarette sales. The raise was substantial, Phoenix wasn't hell. Man plans, God laughs.

Chapter Seventeen

Movements

"**D**ave, I was sorry to hear about your divorce. You doing alright?"

The phone call was from former Captain, now trial attorney, Horatio Barnes ("H" to his friends), one of which I was lucky enough to call myself.

"Mostly," I answered truthfully. I was actually rather surprised at how quickly I had gotten over my divorce from Em. The occasional attack of loneliness was offset by an increasing sense of freedom, in decisions, career and personal, public and private. I wondered if this was normal, but normal wasn't something you could check out very much in Southern California where divorce was more of an inevitable ritual than a personal catastrophe. I had come to realize that Em and I were more an exercise in respectability than a passionate love affair. We cared for and respected one another but there always seemed to be a part missing, a part I would search for the rest of my life.

"I want you to call someone," "H" continued, "He's heading up a veteran movement you should consider becoming a part of."

I was all ears.

"His name is Shad Mehan, he's spearheading a movement to establish storefront Counseling Centers for Vietnam

Veterans, a part of the Veterans Administration, but separate, off site, staffed by Vietnam vets who do peer counseling, community outreach, at street level, that kind of stuff," "H" explained.

"About time," was all I could think of to say. The worst kept secret in America was the ongoing, disgraceful depiction and treatment of Vietnam veterans since the war's end. Much like my, "What kind of drugs did you use?" experience, Vietnam vets were commonly viewed as "ticking time bombs," malcontents and losers whether on TV, in the movies, or on the nightly news. The Veterans Administration largely shunned the younger, angrier, more troubled Vietnam veterans in favor of the aging, complacent, respected veterans of World War 2 and Korea.

"So, who is this guy, Mehan?" I asked skeptically, having stopped believing in saviors a long time ago.

"He was a Psych Officer in Nam, one of the Good Guys. I met him at an Agent Orange symposium in D.C. last year. He's trying to get the funding to open these Vet Centers across the country. He's looking for staff, I thought of you."

"I'm in!" I decided, somewhat prematurely.

"Hey, I'm not hiring you, he would be. He's in LA, give him a call, take my name in vain, let me know what happens."

I got all the pertinent information from "H", caught up on his life and adventures, expounded a bit on my ups and downs, and promised to keep in touch. Then I called this Shad guy, hoping saviors hadn't gone completely out of style.

"Twins! You're telling me that that woman in there, my wife, has given us two baby boys and is now sleeping like a baby herself?!" LT was flabbergasted, in a good way, as he spoke with the Homer based pediatrician and friend Janice Lamare.

"Sedated is the word we like to use, LT. She had a busy night, as you well know. Now you should go get sedated yourself and come back here in eight hours and meet your sons."

Sons.

The word would not leave LT's mind as he walked from the clinic to the VFW hall in the early morning light. Coffee - no coffee with - was in order. Annie, two sons, a community in which he was loved and respected, meaningful work and good health. What else could he ask for? As the sunlight filled his soul.

"Congratulations are in order I understand," Alaska State Trooper Luke Drayber proclaimed as LT entered the veteran's hall to a hearty round of approval from the rest of the early morning breakfast crowd.

"Twins, Luke! Two boys, can you believe it?" LT boasted and marveled.

"Belief will only take you so far, LT. When do we meet these rascals?"

"I haven't met them yet, Luke. Saw them through the glass window and got sent home, or here, actually."

"The calm before the storm, my friend. You'll have your hands full soon enough," Luke proclaimed as LT's steaming hot mug of coffee arrived at the table.

"How's Annie?" Luke asked.

"Unconscious but smiling," LT replied.

The conversation continued as it seemed like half the town stopped by their table to offer congratulations.

As the friendship filled his soul.

"This will change our lives forever and ever," Margaret Mary exclaimed, not a little saddened by the prospect.

"Yes, but life is change no?" Gianna replied as they sat sipping wine on the veranda of their home.

"But Switzerland is so far away," Margaret Mary responded.

"Six hours only, you have been, we have been, and Thanh loved the trip."

The discussion centered on Thanh's opportunity to attend an elite boarding school in Montreux, Switzerland. She had been accepted after a rigorous screening process, both academic and familial, to one of the finest private schools in the world.

"So far away," Margaret Mary mused, as so many of her loved ones were.

"It is as Sister Beatrice said, 'We have given her wings, now she must fly.'"

"I will miss her so badly," Margaret Mary whispered.

"As will I," Gianna reasoned, "but this is best for her, a rare opportunity. We give them a child, they educate a woman, the best she can be."

"Thanh wants this?" Margaret Mary asked for the hundredth time.

"She does," Gianna answered, "and this is best for her."

"As we always promised," Margaret Mary answered, and the decision was made.

Kevin, not Butchie, saw her at the bus stop every morning. He did not know her name. He was afraid to ask. He watched her out of the corner of his eye, shyly glancing away if she noticed. He thought she was pretty. He didn't think she would ever care what he thought.

Susan Waltz noticed Kevin as well. He always sat alone, at the far end of the shelter bench, seldom looked up, always looked lonely. Susan was twenty-six, single and lived at home with her parents. She worked at the Lowell Public Library, assistant to the assistant librarian. She didn't think Kevin even knew she was alive. Until today.

"Miss, does this belong to you?"

As Susan boarded the bus that morning she dropped a mitten, a simple, homemade, knitted yellow mitten. Kevin picked it up and returned it to her. And two lives were going to change for the much, much better.

She smiled and said thank you. Kevin went to his ususal seat in the back of the bus. Susan sat up front but halfway to downtown she turned and smiled at Kevin. Kevin smiled back and found himself getting off the bus two stops early, at the Lowell Public Library. He could walk the rest of the way. They stood next to one another on the city sidewalk.

"Thank you for returning my mitten," Susan said.

Kevin nodded and started to walk away.

"You didn't say you're welcome," Susan whispered to Kevin's back. He heard. He stopped and turned. "You're welcome very much," he stammered and hurried on his way. It was a start.

"I thought they'd be taller." LT said, holding white roses and baby blue balloons. Annie was blissfully cradling two sleeping baby boys, one under each arm, in her hospital bed.

"Do NOT, NOT make me laugh," Annie groaned, "If you ever expect to lay a conjugal hand on me ever again do not make jokes. I am sore, and hungry and the happiest I have ever been in my life." She finally smiled.

LT laid the roses at the foot of the bed and handed the balloons to the maternity nurse who hovered nearby. "Can I hold them?" he asked.

"Not just yet, Tarzan. Babies sleep now, Mommy eats now. Tarzan goes away, comes back later with a pizza," Annie suggested, as the maternity nurse shook her head an emphatic no.

"What are we going to call them?" LT asked.

"Name them, Daddy, we are going to name them. Right now I'm just calling them Lefty and Righty." She wiggled the appropriate elbow with the babies. "They want me to stay here one more day for rest then we take them home, sit on our front porch and decide what to name our children." Annie's smile widened, so did LT's.

And love filled their souls.

The meeting with Shad Mehan went very well. He was a fiery, fanatical, rapid talking advocate of veterans rights, particularly Vietnam veterans. The heartbreak of our homecoming had affected him deeply on a personal and communal level. There were wrongs to be righted. Shad Mehan was forming the posse to do it. I wanted in.

"Salary-wise I'm not going to be able to even come close to what you're making now," Shad explained as he looked over my application.

"My decision to get involved is not a financial one, Shad."

"Still, it's going to be a major drop in income."

"Might be the best thing for me," I replied, "Money is just not the most important thing in my life."

"You want to stay in Orange County?" Shad asked.

"If possible, but I'm open to a move."

"My team leader down there is Ken Stone. I'll set up a meeting with him and if he approves there is an opening in his Vet Center in Anaheim."

"Let's set it up." I suggested.

And the die was cast. My meeting with Ken Stone went very well and a day or so later I got the call that the job was mine if I wanted it. I now had to make a break from some very nice people at Brown & Williamson tobacco and tighten my belt financially for my new career. Good for me.

"I go to the Dutch Tea Room on Fridays for lunch if you would like to meet me there sometime," Susan offered shyly one morning as she and Kevin got off the bus in downtown Lowell. Smiles had beccome nods, with an occasional "Good morning" between these two shy souls until Susan spoke up and made, what was for her, this daring offer. This was Thursday, Kevin could have a whole day to think the offer over. Instead he swallowed the lump of fear in his throat and said, "Yes, I'd like to do that. What time?"

And the date was made and all the fuss would follow.

Chapter Eighteen

Learnings

When Thanh wasn't smiling happily, she was crying and holding on tight to Margaret Mary and Gianna's hands. The train they were riding rolled through the gorgeous Swiss countryside finally revealing the first view of Lake Geneva, a pristine blue jewel in the valley of the Swiss Alps.

"C'est magnifique, Mamas," She proclaimed looking out the window.

"It was by this lake, many years ago, that Mary Shelley wrote her short stories and her most famous story, that of Frankenstein," Margaret Mary declared, literary, as always.

"And Charlie Chaplin, the 'little tramp' you so adore also lived here, died here, in his chateau by the lake," Gianna added. "Many famous people, artists, actors, musicians and painters have come here to live and study. As now you shall study here and perhaps become famous as well."

"I don't want to be famous; I want to be with you," Thanh answered.

"And you wanted the best school for your education. Here is the best school," Margaret Mary reasoned. "We will be together, Thanh. Gianna and I will come to visit as often as we can, and you shall take this train home whenever there is a vacation from your school," She added as the train pulled into the station. As the train hissed to a stop the conductor swung open the carriage doors and announced, "Geneva, Lake Geneva, Montreaux, bienvenue."

And in their small carriage compartment nobody moved. This was going to be a time of goodbyes. Reception and registration at the boarding school, hugs and kisses at the dormitory and then farewells as Margaret Mary and Gianna boarded the return train to Paris. Thanh would remain, a new student starting a new life.

"I'm frightened, Mamas," Thanh whispered.

"Change is always a little frightening, Thanh, this change will be very good for you, part of your growing up," Gianna offered.

"And part of our growing older," Margaret Mary added, smiling and not smiling, together and at once.

As they walked, arm in arm in arm, to the registrar's office the beauty of the campus, the lake, the mountains, raised their spirits and their hopes for the happiness to come from this parting.

"It's time, big guy, Lefty and Righty need names," Annie proclaimed while sitting happily on their front porch two days after leaving the hospital. "It was only your juice as town constable that allowed us take them home without them."

"I've been giving this a lot of thought," LT answered, "and the guys down at the Legion hall have been very helpful. We took a vote."

"You took a what?" Annie asked.

"A vote, we voted on names for the boys."

"I can hardly wait to hear this," Annie sighed.

"Okay, Lefty, due to his swarthy good looks and obvious musical talent, should be Elvis Wolfgang Baker. Righty, the more sensitive, but smarter of the two, should be Hondo Einstein Baker. So say all of us from the Legion Hall. Elvis W and Hondo E for short."

Annie was trying not to gag on her chablis and countered patiently, "You are not embracing this whole parenthood thing quite yet, are you dear?"

LT dropped the tomfoolery. "Actually I was hoping we could name one of our sons after my Dad and the other after your father."

Annie acknowledged the sincerity in LT's suggestion and countered, "I think naming one of our children after your father is a fine idea. Your father raised you, loved you. My father didn't raise me, he capitalized me. He was never there when I needed him, only his money was." Sadness was in Annie's voice as she said this. "I have given this some thought as well," she continued, "I think Jacob, after the man who left us this home and became your redeemer would be a better choice."

"Robert and Jacob," LT smiled, "I like it, I like it a lot. What about the middle names?"

"I thought of that too," Annie replied, "Why not let them decide? Say on their twelfth birthday we let them choose their own middle names?"

"Like Elvis or Hondo?" LT grinned.

"Like whatever they choose, hopefully not Elvis or Hondo."

And the matter was settled and the paperwork completed.

"Save Yourself, Lifeguard."

The class instructor, Bill Mahoney, wrote in very large letters on the blackboard. Then he turned to face us, the counselors in training for the brand new, freshly launched Vet Center program.

"Each of you better take a long, hard look at that sentence," he announced, "Because if any of you think you're here to save somebody else and not yourself as well, you are badly mistaken and I will not have it."

Silence filled the room along with reverence and some individual sense of foreboding. "Help Without Hassles" was the Outreach Program's slogan for working with Vietnam veterans. Salvaging them from the neglect and vilification most had experienced upon their coming home from

Vietnam was our mission. Saving ourselves while doing so was a program priority. There were twenty four of us in the classroom, newly hired Outreach Counselors with little clue as to the rigors and hardships we were about to face.

"All of you are Vietnam veterans," Shad Mehan interjected, "you all served at least one tour in Vietnam, that is part of the reason you were hired. It is also the reason you are going to have to take a very hard look at yourselves if you want to survive in this program."

Bill took a seat on the front edge of his desk. In a softer voice he continued, "Nobody got out of Vietnam without being impacted by the experience. I don't care what you did, or didn't do while you were in country. Being in-country was enough. Michael Herr was a correspondent for Esquire magazine during the war. He wrote about what he saw and felt and lived in his excellent book, 'Dispatches.' Those of you who haven't read it, read it. Those of you who have will recognize what I'm going to read. He began…

…All the same, one place or another, it was always going on, rock around the clock, we had the days, and he had the nights. You could be in the most protected space in Vietnam and still know that your safety was provisional, that early death, blindness, loss of legs, arms, or balls, major and lasting disfigurement-the whole rotten deal-could come in on the freaky-fluky as easily as in the so-called expected ways; you heard of so many of these stories, it was a wonder anyone was left alive to die in firefights and mortar-rocket attacks.

After a few weeks, when the nickel had jarred loose and dropped, I saw that everyone around me was carrying a gun, I also saw that any one of them could go off at any time, putting you where it wouldn't matter whether it had been an accident or not. The roads were mined, the trails booby-trapped, satchel charges and grenades blew up jeeps and movie theatres, the V.C. worked inside all the camps as shoeshine boys and laundresses and honey-dippers; they'd starch your fatigues and burn your shit and go home and mortar your area. Saigon and Cholon and Danang held such hostile vibes that you felt you were being dry-sniped every time someone looked at you, and choppers fell out of the sky like fat poisoned birds.

Bill put the book aside. "What I'm trying to tell you here, what Mr. Herr is telling you here, is that NOBODY got out of Nam without being wounded, inside or outside. Not all wounds show. If any of you think you got through your tour without being psychologically affected by it, you are sadly, and tragically mistaken. If you are going to survive in this job, you are going to have to deal with that wound. Yours first, before you can help others."

I swallowed hard, thinking of the 571st Dustoff. I didn't want a lot of eye contact with those around me but couldn't help but notice the room had become grim and very silent. Then Bill said, "Let's get started."

"This," he announced holding up another book, "is the Diagnostic and Statistical Manual of the American Psychiatric Association. It is called, for short, DSM-III. There have been, as you might have guessed, two previous editions of this book. This edition has something new, something that pertains to us. It is called 'Post Traumatic Stress Disorder.' Simply put PTSD, as we will call it, means a symptomatic reaction to a traumatic experience that is outside the range of normal human experience."

"You call that 'simply put?'" Marcus Canby, one of the new counselors, asked to the general amusement of the room.

Bill Mahoney got the joke. "Look you guys, eggheads love using big words. Eggheads wrote the DSM-III, they also oversee the VA's Outpatient Psychiatry system. The eggheads don't like us, we aren't as credentialed as they are, we don't use the big words they use, we probably won't wear a tie to work, but…we were in-country as most of them were not. Events that were 'outside the range of normal human experience' were everyday occurrences for us. This program is about peer counseling, not egghead labeling, but we have got to learn the lingo to get along with them."

"How's that working out so far?" Marcus again, a natural skeptic.

"You don't have to worry about that," Bill answered, "that's my job and Shad's. I want you guys on the streets, in the woods, the boonies, the jails, finding the guys who don't trust the eggheads, don't trust the VA and are suffering as a result of their Vietnam service."

"Some of you Team Leaders are going to lock horns with the VA over our mission, try to get along with them. They're skeptical, let's change that," Shad added.

"Let's get back to this PTSD thing," Bill said, "a little history is in order. Back in World War 1 psychiatric combat casualties were thought to have 'shell shock,' some kind of concussive disorder from being around heavy artillery. This didn't work out so well because many of the mental breakdowns occurred with soldiers not necessarily exposed to artillery shelling, the cause was misunderstood, but the label stuck. In World War 2 the name for psychiatric breakdowns became 'Combat fatigue.' 25 % of the soldiers medically evacuated from combat zones were diagnosed with 'Combat fatigue,' 50% of the medical discharges were for psychiatric disorders."

"That's a lot of fatigue," Tom Washburn, another of the new counselors suggested.

"It was also a lot of mis-diagnosed bull shit," Bill continued. "Soldiers in war break down for lots of reasons, most of them pretty horrible. That is the inevitable nature of war. During the Korean War they called Combat Fatigue 'the thousand yard stare,' a trance-like state observed in soldiers after prolonged exposure to combat. Nobody knew much about what to do about it, but the occurrences seemed to be increasing."

"Some observers believed that the higher levels of education, intelligence, and sensivity of the average soldier contributed to the intolerance of combat stressors," Shad added.

"The French have a term for this disorder I particularly like," Bill added, 'Le Coeur de Soldat,' it means, 'soldier's heart,' a poetic rendering of PTSD."

"Simply stated of course," Marcus Canby said.

"It's nice they have so many phrases to describe what's wrong with us," Tom Washburn commented, "Any news on how we can get better?" Bitterness bled through the sarcasm; truth embellished the reply.

"I truly believe," Shad said, "that we are going to be the answer, or at least an important part of that answer. Peer counseling, talking it out among ourselves, mutual support and understanding, role modeling the proper behavior, that is what we are all about, and I know that means asking a lot of all of you."

"Which brings us to another point, you will all be fighting the negative stereotype of the Vietnam veteran. Drug user, hippie, malcontent, loser." Bill didn't sound happy as he ticked off the more common adjectives associated with Vietnam veterans. "In fact, the Vietnam War had the highest rate of enlistees of any war this country has ever fought. 75% of the US casualties in Nam were volunteers. There were 238 Medals of Honor awarded in Vietnam and over 300,000 Purple Hearts. How many of you served more than one tour in Vietnam?" Several hands were raised, including my own. "Multiple tours were voluntary. Anybody want to say why they served a second tour?"

"For my brothers," Marcus Canby answered, "right thing to do, right place to do it."

Heads nodded.

"Anybody else? Bill asked.

"Flying Dustoff was the finest thing I have ever done in my life," I heard myself saying, "I was proud to be doing it."

More heads nodded and that old, familiar lump in my throat returned to strangle me quietly.

"You people are going to be the vanguard, the image changers, role models for the veterans you will come in contact with. That is why it is essential that you deal with your own issues first. You will be held to a higher standard, randomly tested for drugs and alcohol by the VA, watched, scrutinized, evaluated. Your failure will harm this program, I cannot allow that," Shad added.

The room grew somber once again, quiet, reflective, attentive.

"How bad is the VA out to get us?" Another of the counselor-trainees, whose name I couldn't remember asked.

"Not as bad as you might think," Shad answered, "There are some forward thinkers among them. We've got Art Blank and Max Cleland on our side, several of the hospital heads are willing to give us a chance and we've got each other."

"Does everybody at the VA get tested for drugs and alcohol?" Marcus asked.

"They can be, as government employees its part of the deal. But we are in the ten ring, a little more suspect, a little less trusted," Bill replied.

"Substance abuse is going to be an issue," Shad admitted. "If you smoke pot and test positive or drive drunk and get caught, they can fire you just like any other employee. But if one of you gets busted, we all get busted."

Which gave us all something else to think about. I never liked pot much, tried it in Nam, was around it in college, but pot was not for me. I could catch a good buzz off a proper cabernet though and a cold beer on a hot day was always on my list. Now getting buzzed or high was going to impact others as well as myself and as I looked around the room, I could see that I was not the only one processing this.

"Now let's talk about this PTSD business," Bill said as he wrote, in large letters, on the blackboard:

Recurrent and intrusive distressing recollections of parts of your service in Vietnam.

Recurrent distressing dreams of the event, or events.

Sudden acting or feeling that the distressing event was recurring.

Intense psychological distress at exposure to events that symbolize or resemble an aspect of the traumatic event, including anniversary dates.

"Write these down people, we are going to be talking about them a lot." Bill rested his chalk and retook his seat at the front of the desk. "These are signposts, indicators that something is amiss, that PTSD may be a serious and disturbing issue in your life. Anyone in here want to tell me they have never had any of these reactions?"

Nobody spoke up.

"I didn't think so," Bill concluded.

"Here are a few more behaviors to be aware of," Shad added, taking the chalk from Bill and writing:

Efforts to avoid thoughts or feelings associated with the trauma.

Efforts to avoid activities or situations that arouse recollections of the trauma.

Inability to recall an important aspect of the trauma.

"Eggheads call this one 'psychogenic amnesia,'" Shad commented, "think of it as blocking shit out you don't want to deal with."

He continued writing.

Markedly diminished interest in significant activities.

Feeling of detachment or estrangement from others.

Restricted range of affect.

"That's feeling emotionally numb or stuck to you non-eggheads," Shad said as his writing went on.

Sense of foreshortened future.

"One day at a time, not in a good way," Shad said as this list became more personal and more fitting for me and for a lot of other guys in the room.

Difficulty falling asleep or staying asleep.

Outbursts of anger or irritability.

Difficulty concentrating.

Hypervigilance.

Exaggerated startle response.

"And finally, and you are going to love this one," Shad said as he wrote,

Physiological reactivity upon exposure to events that symbolize or resemble an aspect of the traumatic event.

"You mean like panicking in all the wrong places?" Marcus asked.

"That's exactly what I mean," Shad replied and rested his chalk.

"Lock in gentlemen, we have a lot of work to do," Bill concluded as the writing on the wall sank in.

Our Outreach Counselor training went on for an entire week. Besides classroom work we broke down into small groups and discussed our own issues, or own recollections and our own trauma. Thoughts were exchanged, memories were shared, tears fell as we came together as a team.

I had made a concentrated effort in my life so far not to think a lot about Vietnam. I stayed busy, went to school, played cowboy on the Texas border, married, careered, made big bucks and bigger mistakes. Now it seemed I had to take a few steps back before I could go any further forward. Up to now my life felt like I was being swept along in a river of conformity, doing what I thought I should do without giving much consideration to the value of what I was doing. Deep down inside I knew this job was going to change that.

The Vet Center concept was simple, bring the Veterans Administration services to the veterans they had shunned, the Vietnam veterans. We would work out of storefront offices, with street smart, in-country, veteran peer counselors, offering help without hassles, respect and understanding, without judgments.

There would initially be eighty-seven Vet Centers across the country with more to come as personnel could be trained and results could be evaluated. The Vet Center Program was initially given a two-year window of performance. It would then be reevaluated and likely closed down. I was assigned to the Anaheim Vet Center located at 859 South Harbor Boulevard about a mile and a half north of the main gate of Disneyland. Ironic, but proper. My journey was about to begin.

Sitting across from one another at the Dutch Tea Room neither Kevin or Susan could think of much to say. Both were locked into their own shyness, their own loneliness.

"Is your coffee okay?" Kevin asked.

"Tea, I have tea," Susan responded.

"Tea, I meant tea. Is it okay?"

"Yes."

And then they stared at each other some more.

"I'm sorry," Kevin finally admitted, "I'm not very good at this."

"Well," Susan answered, "You did guess what I was drinking in only two guesses."

And her joke and her smile began to melt the ice surrounding Kevin, not Butchie.

They exchanged back stories, guarded past histories, generic tales of growing up in Lowell. Kevin did not talk about the Navy, Susan did not speak of being abandoned by a fiance, or of her wedding that never took place. Kevin only came to life when he spoke of his niece, Samantha and of the kids he coached at the gym. Susan spoke of her love for Hampton Beach in not so far away New Hampshire and of her Siamese cat, Maise, with whom she shared her deepest secrets.They talked of simple things, things that did not hurt. An hour passed quickly before Susan announced she had to get back to work. Kevin too was overdue at the gym.

"Maybe we could have lunch again some time," Kevin asked, "if you want to I mean."

"I'd like that," Susan answered. "When?"

"Whenever you want," Kevin said, "I come down-city every day except Sunday, but we could do it on Sunday too, if you want." Kevin was trying not to sound too anxious, and failing.

Susan laughed her very relaxing and charming smile. "Sunday would be nice, we wouldn't have to hurry back to work."

And a day, THE date, was set, and all the fuss followed.

"Sixteen-five, Eddie. Nice work."

Max Mechan, the Golden Palace sports book manager stacked the cash on the desk in front of Eddie. "We booked $165,000 on those college parties you threw. Ten percent is you."

Eddie had kept his own track of the numbers, $185,000 was more accurate, but he figured it was best not to quibble. "Most of it is still in markers, no?" Eddie asked.

"Let us worry about the markers, Eddie. You did good. You're back on the line Monday morning."

Sixteen grand plus for six weeks work was good, very good, Eddie figured as he picked up his cash. Eddie had hosted four Homecoming Football Kegger parties for well to do alumni from several Ivy League institutions of higher learning. Doctors, lawyers and dentists making too much money and drinking too much beer tended to bet loyally and generously on home teams. In four of the six games Eddie hosted the betting line was dead on, dead against the home team and very lucrative for the book makers. The remaining two games were also close, close enough that a lot of money changed hands, mostly into Eddie's.

"You good at anything else, Eddie?" Max asked.

"I shoot a pretty good game of nine ball." Eddie boasted.

"I got guys so good at nine ball they'd make you cry. You ever play any golf?"

Eddie hadn't. "How'd ya' like to take a few lessons? I've got an idea." Max countered and explained.

I'm goin' golfin', Eddie mused as he left Max's office. Wait till Ma hears about this.

Chapter Nineteen

Beginnings

"If we are going to keep coming here one of us is going to have to get a driver's license," Susan said as they got off the Greyhound Bus from Lowell to Hampton Beach. A forty-minute car ride was a two-hour bus trip and both she and Kevin agreed on the solution.

"I will if you will," Kevin volunteered.

"If you will I won't have to," Susan answered as they walked along the boardwalk. What had begun as a wintertime romance had become a summer love for both of them. They made plans, wished wishes and discussed practicalities.

"A driver's license won't be much good without a car," Kevin said.

"Then we'll have to get one," Susan answered.

"We," thought Kevin for the first time in a very long while.

"You never told me why you don't drive a car," Susan said.

"I didn't think I'd need one," Kevin answered.

"That's not true," Susan said, "You used to own one, a white convertible, a Pontiac."

"How do you know that? Kevin asked.

"I looked you up, I'm a librarian, remember? Your picture was in the Lowell Sun lots of times. You were a boxer, one of the pictures was of you leaning against your car. The picture named you as Butchie and said you were a Golden Gloves champion."

"I sold that car when I went into the Navy," Kevin, now Butchie, replied.

"I saw that too. The story said you went into the Navy and were in submarines! I always wanted to ride in a submarine," Susan declared.

Kevin became wary, cautious. Embarrassed. This was new ground, something they had not discussed before. Something Kevin had never really discussed before. Susan noticed the change, took hold of Kevin's arm.

"Did something bad happen to you in the Navy?" She asked.

"Kind of," Kevin squirmed under the question.

"If it did, I want to know about it. I have to know about it," Susan declared.

And just like that Kevin felt the ice again, thick, heavy, all around him, stacking up between himself and Susan. Fittingly, he froze.

"Kevin, you have your secrets, I have my secrets. Three years ago, my fiancé left me standing at the altar in the Sacred Heart church on my wedding day while he ran off to California. That is why I live at home with my parents and why my father is ashamed of me and why I have never brought you over to their house to meet my parents That is one of my secrets, my biggest shame. I need you to talk to me about yours, please."

"He left you at the altar?"

"In the church full of people, my family, his family, all our friends. Afterward I thought I would never stop crying. I thought I was worthless, so did my father. He still does. I don't feel worthless anymore, not since I met you. Is your secret worse than that?"

Kevin didn't know how to answer. Her father thinks she's worthless. Her fiancé ran off and left her? She thought she'd never stop crying?

"I need to be sitting down when I tell you this," Kevin said as Susan led him to a boardwalk bench.

"We're sitting, and I love you," Susan offered.

Kevin was strangling on his words but the "I love you" helped a lot.

"I was assigned to the USS Pargo, a nuclear submarine. We were going on a secret mission under the Arctic Ice. We were to stay beneath the ice for one month to test equipment and eavesdrop on Russian communications."

Kevin started to twist and squirm on the bench. He's getting to the hard part, the secret part, Susan thought and took his hand into hers.

"We were under the ice a week when it happened. One morning I couldn't get out of my bunk. I was petrified; I felt like all the ice was crushing me. Where we were the ice was a mile thick above us, a whole mile!"

Kevin had a faraway look in his eyes now, he was not on a boardwalk bench at Hampton Beach, he was under a mile of ice in the Arctic Sea.

"They took me to sick bay because I couldn't get out of my bunk. I was scared, Susan, terrified, panicking, I felt like I was going to die.

Susan didn't speak, just held his hand a little tighter.

"The Navy wasn't about to cancel a top-secret mission just because of me so they gave me some meds to calm down. They didn't work so they gave me more meds, bigger doses. They kept me in sick bay, giving me meds for the whole three weeks we were under the ice. They gave so many pills I didn't know where I was anymore. When we got back to port, they put me in the Naval hospital in Connecticut, on the psych ward. Finally, they discharged me and sent me to a VA hospital in Boston, on the psych ward again. Only my mother and sister knew where I was until two guys I know found me."

"What do you mean they found you?"

"I'm not sure anymore, but they kept coming to see me, so did my sister and my Mom. Finally, I started going home on weekends and Dave and Ted, they are the guys who found me, kept coming to visit. We boxed together a long time ago. They helped me, my sister and mother helped me, and I got the job at the gym, but I'm still so ashamed."

"Ashamed of what, exactly?" Susan asked.

"Of being a coward," Kevin finally admitted.

"I'm going to tell you something and I don't want you to get mad at me, or anyone else, okay?" Susan said. "I talked to your sister about this, she told me about you in the hospital. She said the Navy admitted they over-medicated you and intensified your breakdown. She said it wasn't your fault, but you won't stop thinking it is."

"Breakdown," Kevin choked.

"Yes breakdown, Kevin. You don't think I broke down when that asshole left me standing at the altar? Breakdowns happen, Kevin, they can happen to anyone. Having a breakdown is hard, getting better is harder."

"I never heard you swear before," Kevin replied.

"You'll hear more than that if we get to talking about Jimmy. You know what that asshole did? He decided he was gay when he went to California, and he told his parents it was my fault because I wouldn't sleep with him before we got married!" Susan was steaming. Kevin was trying to keep a straight face.

"You were engaged to a fag?"

"Don't start with me Butchie the Boxer!" She exclaimed then leaned in for a massive hug. They both chuckled inside at how ridiculous life was and how comical it could become. The rest was just healing each other.

The Anaheim Vet Center opened in the fall of 1981. We were given a two-year mandate by the Veterans Administration, sink or swim, prove whether the concept of street level counseling worked or not. There were four of us on the Vet Center team, initially. Ken Stone was my Team Leader, boss and friend. Al Villow was the other counselor, a recovering alcoholic who had been badly wounded in Vietnam. Al used a cane, and his right arm was crippled. War wounds, the outside ones. Janice, our secretary, would do as much counseling as the rest of us greeting the Vietnam veterans who began showing up at the Center.

"This the Vietnam vet place?" The cautious, hesitant man in the doorway asked before stepping into the center.

"It will be," Janice answered, "as soon as you come in."

That was vet number one, the first guy to visit. More followed, curious or cranky, quiet or loud, willing or unwilling. And then the stories started.

One man who came in lost both his brothers in Vietnam. He was not a veteran; he was a sufferer. Another spent his entire tour in Vietnam washing blood out of convoy trucks, blood and body parts, every day. He wanted to know why.

Another was a Military Policeman in Saigon, prey to the enemy, distrusted and feared by the friendlies, shunned and separated from the rest of us, alone with a badge and gun. He lived behind a heavy beard, biker leathers and a broken heart.

Wives of alcoholic husbands came in, desperate for help. Druggies, street and preppie versions, came in looking for help. Beggars and bosses, thieves and clergymen, all Vietnam veterans with a story to tell that nobody, until now, wanted to listen to, arrived. We listened.

These are the words of Albert Dobbs, a Vietnam vet who was serving a two-year sentence in a Louisiana prison for "attempted armed robbery" when he came to the attention of the Vet Center. A team of experts and legal counsel intervened on his behalf and Albert was subsequently released into my custody for counseling at the Anaheim Vet Center. Albert related…

> **"I shot an entire family of people, not for what they did, but because they happened to be in the area where seventeen of my friends had been slaughtered. Now I see these people just as clearly, every night as I did on that day, and they are just as real as I am, and they watch me at night. If I am a thousand years old, I'll never forget that day and I'll never forget those faces, and now, when it rains, I smell death."**

Albert persevered at the Center for two months. He lived in a hallway house, struggled to find work and stay sober until one day he disappeared, in the wind. A lot of vets did that. A lot more didn't.

In the weeks and months after the Vet Center opened, I heard more of these stories, many more, too many more. So did Ken Stone and Allen Villow. We started to crack, overwhelmed by the oceans of despair and misery we heard every day. We sat in our own counsel, team meetings, debriefs and soul searches. I started to drink privately, quietly, by myself. More vets poured into our center as the word spread that we could and would help. Soon there were too many of them and not enough of me. But I was getting better at hiding it.

"So how do you like being a Dad?" Alaska State Trooper Luke Drayber asked his very fatigued looking buddy, LT.

"Do babies ever sleep?" LT asked partly cuious, partly in despair.

Luke laughed. LT groaned.

"I don't know how Annie does it," he continued, "she's so patient with them, so…loving. Some nights I just want to put them out on the back porch and let them howl."

"Comes with the territory Dad," Jake grinned. "How about when they're not howling?"

"Elvis is great, Hondo is the same. They hold hands together when Annie puts them in the same crib.

Whatever one does, the other follows. I'm teaching Elvis the words to 'Suspicious Minds' and Hondo looks like he's solving equations in his head."

"They're only six months old LT, 'Suspicious Minds' may be a little advanced. you should try 'Love Me Tender.'" Luke knew of which he spoke, he and his wife had three boys, wild, wooly and wonderful.

"I do you know," LT said, "'Love them Tender.' They are all I think about. I see how happy they make Annie, and feel how happy they make me. I just wish they would sleep a little longer."

"Good luck with that. Annie alright?"

"She's terrific, no sleep, overworked, a million chores and she glows. Go figure."

"Figuring women is not my job. You going up to Owl Creek today?"

"Yeah, meeting Mike up there to clean up a clog or two, run off some beavers."

"Sounds exciting."

'Exciting I've got at home, Luke, and howling, and there's TWO of them!"

"Nice putt, Eddie, almost." The banker from Kansas City chuckled as Eddie missed the hole, but not by much. Eddie dropped the tap-in, staying true to his 18 handicap and role in the foursome.

Eddie was the stringer, the guy who kept the match close while his partner, Bob Lehigh, parred every hole with an occassional birdie or two to keep the duo's lead. Eddie and Bob played partners at the Las Vegas Country Club, filling out foursomes with vacationing players and quietly establishing two teams, one healthy bet, and an assured victory. But not by much.

This was Max's master plan. Eddie was a quick learner, good hand and eye coordination and after a dozen or so lessons, a natural stringer. He jollied up the match, stayed close and let Bob close the bet. A couple hundred a round, side bets, double or nothing, eigtheen holes, maybe thirty six on the weekend, Max's plan was working and about to go big time.

"They went for twelve grand?" Even Max was surprised.

"Six each, nine holes and they quit," Eddie said.

"And they paid," Bob added.

"We are going to take this to another level," Max explained, "There's a tournament, kind of celebrity-am, low key, good money affair up at Tahoe next weekend. Top twenty finishers get paid. You two are in."

"Tahoe," Eddie thought, "maybe I'll take Ma." And he did.

The next weekend Eddie, his mother and his aunt Cam were enjoying the Cal Neva Lodge on the south shore of Lake Tahoe. The golf tournament was to begin Saturday morning at the Edgewood Golf Course. Friday night was the Cal Neva buffet and Keno Marathon for Ma and her sister, Auntie Cam, while Eddie and Bob hustled celebs and amateurs alike in the lounge.

"No! No! No!" Eddie mumbled as his tee shot on nine caught the wind and floated toward the green. Bouncing twice, the ball rolled directly into the hole. An ace, a hole in one. Eddie was pissed. He didn't want to look at his partner, Bob, as the crowd cheered. He knew Bob would have to dump at least five shots on the back nine to make up for this. Dumping was hard for Bob, not so much for Eddie.

Eddie was trying hard to grin as he held aloft the Champion's trophy after the last round. He and Bob had decided it would have been more difficult to have Bob have to dump than for Eddie to have the round of his life. Two birdies and an eagle by Eddie on the back nine sealed the deal. Twenty-five grand to them as winners plus lots of photographs. After the ceremony, in the lounge, Bob couldn't keep himself from laughing. "You should have seen it Max, Eddie's shot is rolling for the hole and he's mumblling 'NO! No! No!' The umpire kind of looks at him funny and Eddie says, 'I thought it was heading for the beach!'"

"I'm not paying you two to win tournaments," Max lamented, "fifth is best, third okay, but not first! Eddie, they're maybe gonna lower your handicap to like a twelve after this. Makes it harder to book bets."

Even so, Max was amused. Life was good, hustling was fun. What could go wrong, again?

"But she is never here when she's here," Margaret Mary lamented.

"Mon couer, she is fourteen, she has a boyfriend and this is Paris!" Gianna replied.

Thanh was home from school, summer recess, three weeks. Margaret Mary and Gianna were seeing less and less of their daughter.

"Where would you be, if you were her?" Gianna added.

"Probably at the library," Margaret Mary admitted, being such a nerd. Just then Thanh breezed into the room, happy and smiling, bringing hugs for all.

"Mamas. We can go tomorrow to Versailles? And Steven can come with us?" Thanh asked.

Steven, of course, was the boyfriend. Friendly, pimpled, awkward and appropriate.

"Of course, if it is all right with his parents," Gianna answered and Margaret Mary agreed.

"They wish to come too," Thanh added, "To meet you as well."

"The 10AM train then? We can meeet them at the station," Margaret Mary proposed. And the date was on. And soon the tears began.

The meeting at the train station was formal and cold. At first sight the parents of pimply Stephan appeared haughty and aloof. When they came to understand that Margaret Mary and Gianna were a couple they became openly disdainful.

"You are lesbians then, I assume?" Stephan's father, Henry Bachon, snorted while his wife sneered.

Margaret Mary was shocked, Gianna outraged. Never before in Paris society or anywhere else had they been snubbed or insulted in any way due to their relationship. This was happening in front of Thanh, who neither understood, nor recognized their attitude. Through all this young Stephan held back, hiding partially behind his mother's considerable bundle of skirts. He would not look Thanh in the eye. Thanh noticed, so did Margaret Mary and Gianna.

"We are as we are, legally married under the law," Gianna replied, seething.

"Not under God's law," Mrs. Bachon, called Berte, added.

"And not in any way that we will have in the life of our son." Henry said as they stormed away towing young Stephan along behind them, ending all conversation.

Margaret Mary was stunned. Gianna was infuriated. Thanh was confused. The day was young.

"Stephan would not look at me," Thanh said as they walked away. "He was hiding behind his mother."

"They did not strike me as kind people, perhaps he is afraid of them," Gianna offered.

"More afraid of them than he cares for me?" Thanh replied.

"Apparently so," Gianna answerd.

"He wore the green hat," Thanh mumbled as she gazed out the train window. Versailles, they reasoned, was as beautiful a place as any to disccus the matter and to Versailles they now travelled.

"I never liked the green hat, but he wore it anyway," Thanh mused.

They were silent for the rest of the train ride. Gianna simmering in her outrage, Margaret Mary watching Thanh as the beautiful French countryside passed by.

Later, while seated in the Versaillles Gardens, Margaret Mary asked, "How did you meet Stephan?"

"He asked me to dance and later he told his friends he liked me and he became my boyfriend," Thanh recalled.

"Did you like him back?" Margaret Mary asked.

Thanh recalled, "He was very polite and I thought if he liked me I was supposed to like him back."

"Even with the green hat?" Gianna interjected helpfully, which got a faint smile from Thanh.

"It was a foolish hat," she answered, "and I told him so, but he would not listen."

Thanh was obiously reflecting, reconsidering her private thoughts of Stephan. "He didn't know who George Gershwin was," She recalled, "and he thought Mozart was a painter."

Margaret Mary tried to conceal a smile, Gianna not so much.

"What did you like about Stephan?" Margaret Mary asked.

"I liked having a boyfriend," Thanh replied simply.

"Perhaps then you should have another," Gianna suggested, and they ordered ice cream.

"And this time I will choose him," Thanh decided to the approval of Margaret Mary and Gianna.

The day in Versailles soothed all the rest.

Chapter Twenty

Outros

Six months after the Vet Center opened I was doing twenty-five to thirty veteran intakes a week, so was Allen, while Ken was limited to ten or fifteen as he fought the bureaucratic battles necessary to keep our doors open. Within six months we had passed our mandate and the two year trial run was extened to six. We did one-on-one counseling, couple's counseling, substance abuse groups, and peer therapy groups. I ran two evening groups a week to acomodate vets who worked full time, and one on Saturday morning to access veterans who could not get to us in the evening. Wives of veterans had their own group run by a Godsend volunteer named Shelly Marr. We were overwhelmed, exhuasted and exhilarated.

Ken Stone called me into his office one February morning just after I got to work.

"I need you to go by the County Jail, Dave. Ask for Sergeant Raponi, he's a Vietnam vet, says there are a couple of vets there maybe we can help."

A "couple" turned out to be a huge understatement. Vietnam vets were being arrested nationwide on a scale far outstripping their civilian peers. Almost twice as many combat veterans were incarcerated upon coming home as non-combat veterans. Somebody had to look into this. In Los Angeles/Orange County this became me.

Subsequently I made my first of many trips to the jails and prisons: Orange County Jail, LA County, the Metropolitan Detention Center, Terminal Island, Wayside, anyplace with bars and guards, and as it turned out, lots of Vietnam vets were in custody. When I met Sergeant Raponi he introduced me to a group of Vietnam vets housed seperately,

"I'm better off in here," one jailhouse vet named Hank told me. "I lose my temper, mess somebody up in here, he probably deserves it. Out there I can't get along any more, when I'm not angry or drunk I feel like I'm going to cry or something. Like I said, I'm better off in here."

"How long are you in for?" I asked another vet.

"Forever, I hope. I'm so sick of being in and out of jail, drunk and lonely, dirty and hungry, this place is three hots and a cot, Dave, and it's where I feel like I belong."

A vet named Tony related, "My second bust was kind of funny. This guy had some kind of machine gun, the thing didn't work and he asks me to take a look at it for him. I'm the bad ass Beret right? So I drive around with this thing in my trunk for two weeks until I get stopped by the cops for driving drunk. They find the gun and I'm history. This Nam vet stuff is getting old. I got two years for hauling that piece of junk around."

Vietnam vets were getting jailed for domestic disputes, drunk and disorderly conduct, drugs, resisting arrest, loitering and homelessness, but mostly they were getting arrested for PTSD. Most of the veterans I found were not criminals. They may have been dependent on drugs or alcohol for self medication, unemployed or unemployable, heartsick, lonely and suffering in the worst possible way, but they, we, were not criminals. We were your children, sent to fight a far-away, unpopular war this country did not want to win then "welcomed" home with disdain and indifference.

This is not a "Get out of jail free" card, or an excuse, it is a root cause, worthy of recognition and treatment along with any appropriate punishment. And it wasn't happening. Figuring out why was my quandry as I visited jail after jail. Lots of these guys were model soldiers, leaders, decorated heroes, Bronze Stars, Silver Stars, Purple Hearts, Air Medals, like my own. The nagging question was, "Could this happen to me?" Their breakdowns could be my own, their histories did not sound remarkeably different from how I felt inside.

I started taking night classes at Cal State Fullerton, working on a Masters Degree in Counseling, looking for tips to do my job better, tips to make me feel better. It wasn't working. I spent a lot of time trying to figure out "Why" Vietnam vets were breaking down in such large numbers and why our own country seemed to hate us. Perspective is everything, even when inaccurate.

Then, in early 1980 one of our Vet Center mentors, Tom Williams, testified before the U.S. Senate Committee on Veterans Affairs and I began to understand. His testimony read in part as he asked...

"If you were demonic and powerful enough to want to make someone "crazy" following a war like Vietnam, what would be the worst set of social, economic, political and psychological conditions you could create for the returnee?

First, you would send a young man fresh out of high school to an unpopular, controversial guerilla war far away from home. Expose him to extremely stressful events, some so horrible that it would be impossible to really talk about them later to anyone except fellow "survivors." To ensure maximal stress, you would create a one year tour of duty during which the combatant flies to and from the war zone singly, without a cohesive, intact, and emotionally supportive unit with high morale.

You would also create a one year rotation to install a "survivor mentality" which would undercut the ideolological commitment to winning the war and seeing it as a noble cause. Then at DEROS (Date of Expected Return from Overseas Service) you would rapidly remove the combatant and singly return him to his front porch without an opportunity to sort out the meaning of the experiences with the men in his unit. No homecoming welcome or victory parades. Ah, but yet, since you are demonic enough, you make sure that the veteran is stigmatized and portrayed to the public as a "drug crazed psychopathic killer." By the virtue of clever selection by the Selective Service system, the veteran would be unable to easily reenter the mainstream of society because he is undereducated and lacks marketable job skills.

Further, since the war itself was so difficult, you would want to make sure that there were no supportive systems in society for him, especially among mental health professionals at VA hospitals who would find his nightmares and residual war related anxieties unintelligible. Finally you would want to establish a GI Bill with inadequate benefits to pay for education and job training, coupled with an economy of high inflation and unemployment.

Last, but not least, you would want him to feel isolated, stigmatized, unappreciated, and exploited for volunteering to serve his country. Tragically, of course, this scenario is not fictitious, it was the homecoming for most Vietnam veterans."

And lots of them were sitting in jail. I worked six days a week, ten, twelve hours a day. Ken and Allen did the same. Both of them were married and our schedule soon began taking a toll on their marriages. My schedule was taking a toll on me. That's when our boss, Regional Director and friend, Shad Mehan, stepped in, "You guys are taking two weeks off, one at a time, one after another. Go, get some rest, regroup. The world will be here when you get back. Ken, you first, then Dave, then Alan. Two weeks, I don't want to see you, hear from you, hear about you."

And that is when I realized I had nowhere to go and no one to be with when I got there. Home wasn't Glenmere Street anymore, hadn't been for a long time. I had lost touch with old friends, failed to make new ones, lived alone and stayed alone. I called my parents, made arrangements to come see them in Florida. I was looking for a sanctuary and knew I could always find one with them. As soon as Ken got back from his two week refresher I was on a plane to Florida.

Helplessly Hoping.

Eileen Margolis entered Peter and Cindy's law office hat in hand, frightened and angry. She faltered, turned to leave when Judy Lawton, the receptionist, asked her why she was there. Eileen steeled herself, turned on her heel and said, "My son has been indecently touched by our parish priest and I want to know if you can do anything about it."

Cindy overheard Eileen's plea from her office and came out front, her heart racing. "What did you say?" Cindy asked.

"I said a priest has molested my son and what are you going to do about it," temper replacing timidity.

"Please come into my office," Cindy said, "Tell me everything. Judy, please call Peter and ask him to get back here right away."

Peter was, in fact, dishing the dirt at the local court house with a coven of local attorneys awaiting their turn before the bench. So far Peter and Cindy's practice was a parade of traffic tickets, domestic disputes, bar brawls and public drunks. Their participation in the national Agent Orange lawsuit had wound down as the nationwide class action procedure wrangeled through a moneteary settlement. All was fun and games at the court house until the pay phone in the hallway rang and "Shank" Duvall, attorney at law, answered.

"Pete! Phone call, your office."

Peter got the "get back here right away" part of the call and hastened to home base. When he arrived Judy waved him into Cindy's office where Eileen was in tears and Cindy was in war paint.

Quick introductions were made as Cindy passed Peter a yellow legal pad filled with angry scribbling. Peter read phrases which disgusted and sickened him: "pulled his pants down to tickle him," "performed oral sex on the boy," "asked the boy to hold his penis and rub it, four separate times, three at the Home, one at the Rectory."

Peter's heart sank. He read, "Father Charles Worthington," in large letters, several times. He looked up from the yellow pad from Cindy to Eileen, he had no words. There were no words.

"How old is your son?" Peter croaked.

"Ten," Eileen answered as another wave of tears and outrage washed over her. "His name is Tommy and he is very ashamed, very frightened."

"Have you taken him to a doctor, or a psychiatrist?" Cindy asked as gently as she could.

"I've taken him nowhere!" Eileen sobbed, "The shame for the world to know?"

"But you have come here," Peter offered, "what would you like us to do?"

A question to which he already knew the answer, and Cindy was already formulating the outcome.

"Stop him!" Eileen shouted, "Keep him away from my son!" Peter set the yellow pad on Cindy's desk and for reasons set deep within himself said a silent prayer for guidance.

"May we talk to the boy?" Cindy asked.

Eileen agreed and Cindy arranged to sit withTommy. After she left Peter called his friend and mentor, Father Scanlon, at the Immaculate Conception church for the most difficult meeting of his life.

And the world turned as a vast tragedy unfolded.

"Annie's taking the boy's down to Santa Barbara for a couple of weeks. I don't know what I'm going to do without them," LT complained to his buddy, Luke Drayber as they shared hot coffee in the cold VFW hall in Homer.

"Get a good night's sleep perhaps?" Luke offered.

"Well, there's that, but the rest, not so much."

"She going down to take care of some business?" Luke asked.

"That, and the cold snap we got coming. Fourteen below is the high for tomorrow."

"Fourteen below is the high for February," Luke said. "Probably a good idea to take 'em down."

"I guess. You know what's weird, Luke? I can't remember what my life was like before they were born, not in a good way, anyway. I miss them when I'm at work, I miss them when I'm here. I'll miss them like crazy when they're gone."

"So take some time, go down there with Annie," Luke offered.

"Can't" LT admitted, "Creeks are going to ice up real bad, Mike won't be able to handle things alone."

"You handled it before Mike got here," Luke replied, "Creeks have been icing up for as long as there have been winters. Never let the job come before your family, LT. Go, be with your boys, be with your wife."

"Maybe I could take a week," LT mused.

"Maybe you could take two, high's supposed to be fifteen come March."

"We could go see my Mom," LT realized.

"You could, you should," Luke answered.

And like Dave, two thousand miles away in Los Angeles, LT, Annie, Lefty (also known by Hondo) and Righty (also known by Elvis), were heading for warmer weather and Florida.

"What will your mother say?" Susan asked over Dutch Tea Room tea.

"I talked to her about it yesterday," Kevin answered, "She said something between hallejuah and good for you both. What about your folks?"

"I haven't said anything yet," Susan replied, "my father will hate it."

"I'm sorry Susan, but your father is an asshole," Kevin whispered.

Susan blushed, as she always did when either of them swore.

"I'm sorry, Sue, I shouldn't have said that."

"But he is," Susan admitted, "you know, what you said he was."

"We should tell him together," Kevin said.

Susan agreed, finished her tea. Her father was in for a big surprise.

"Like hell you will!" Jack Waltz bellowed when Susan and Kevin announced they were moving into an apartment together. "Not without getting married you won't!" He added with equal force.

"Susan and I will get married when she says she is ready to get married, not before," Kevin stated.

"Well I say she's ready now and you two ain't living together until she is." Jack wasn't calming down, Kevin was heating up. Susan intervened.

"Daddy, this is what we are going to do. I will leave tonight if that is what you want, but I am leaving. Kevin and I are going to live together and one day I'm sure we'll get married, but not this day. This is not a request, it is our decision."

Through all this Susan's mother, Barbara, sat quiet and very still. She lived in the ever present shadow of her husband's anger which was generally directed at anything and everything he neither understood nor approved of.

"What have you got to say about all this, you're her mother?" Jack demanded.

"I say it's about time Susan made some decisions for herself and what she chooses to do is none of our business." Susan crossed the room and hugged her mother. Jack's mouth hung open in surprise. Susan and Kevin left her parent's home together hand in hand toward their future.

Margaret Mary looked over her selections one more time.

"I'll take the Benson, the two O'Reilly's and the Cameron," She decided.

"But what about the Drake, the Gautier?" Declan Rourke, the proprietor of the Gallway Gallery asked, "You really should consider them."

"I'll stand by my choices, Declan, not those you feel I should consider," Margaret Mary answered. "We have agreed on the price, please ship them to my gallery in Paris."

Declan signed the bills of sale and Margart Mary left to find Sean and Rose sipping coffee in a nearby café.

"Busines is done!" She announced, joining them at their sunny table. "Thirty paintings in thirty days! I never thought that could happen."

"I've never doubted anything you thought could happen, would happen, daughter. Congratulations!" Sean said.

"And blessings as well," Rose added. "Is not your beautiful daughter going to join us this very day?"

"4PM with Gianna. We must meet them at the airport," Margaret Mary answered.

"And meet them we shall," Sean said. "A fine day for all."

And those were the last words he ever spoke as a car bomb ripped through the Belfast street killing him and Aunt Rose instantly. Margaret Mary was thrown through the plate glass window of the café. She lay bruised and bleeding on the shop floor until the firemen and ambulances arrived. Stabilized and bandaged, she was rushed to the hospital. She was taken out of surgery and placed in the intensive care ward just as Gianna and Thanh's plane landed at the airport.

After two hours of frantic searching and fruitless telephone calls police finally took Gianna and Thanh to the hospital where Margaret Mary was recovering.

"The cuts and bruises are mainly superficial," the doctor explained, "of greater concern are the concussive effects of the explosion. We won't truly be able to assess the damage until she regains consciousness."

"And when will that be?" Gianna asked as Thanh sobbed at her side.

"Sadly, we do not know when, nor do we know if she will," the doctor announced as Thanh's sobs turned to wails and Gianna's heart sank into despair.

"Can we see her?" Gianna asked.

"It is best you do not at this time," the doctor answered. "She needs rest and recovery. Perhaps in a day or so."

Gianna and Thanh checked into a hotel where they heard of yet another car bombing as Belfast bled around them. Terrified, they did not leave the hotel for three days while Margaret Mary slept and recovered. On the fourth day the hospital told them Margaret Mary was conscious and that they could see her. Gianna asked the nurse if Margaret Mary had been told yet of the deaths of her father and Aunt Rose. She had not, and for the present the hospital staff suggested they withhold that news until she was stronger.

Gianna and Thanh rode a cab across the beleagured city carrying their terrible secret. When they entered Margaret Mary's room she was awake and smiling weakly at them.

Are my Da and Rose alright?" she whispered. "They won't tell me anything."

Gianna froze. Thanh turned away. Margaret Mary knew. The great sadness began.

Onward.

THE END

I *f you enjoyed California Dreaming, I would really appreciate a short review, your help in spreading the word is highly valued and reviews make it much easier for readers to find the book.*

To get your FREE copy of BORN ON A MOUNTAINTOP - Book 1 in *The Mountaintop Series:*

Click on the link below to download either PDF or EPUB.

https://shorturl.at/OgcTi

Purchase Paperback on Amazon:
https://www.amazon.com/dp/1513668021

RAISED ON ROCK
(Book Two of *The Mountaintop Series*)

Available from Battle Press, Amazon, Barnes & Noble
and other Booksellers:

https://www.amazon.com/dp/B0CC3MHMY2

https://battlepress.media/?product=raised-on-rock

FORGED IN FIRE
(Book Three of *The Mountaintop Series*):

Available from Battle Press, Amazon, Barnes & Noble
and other Booksellers:

https://www.amazon.com/dp/B0C8Y7Y8XV

https://battlepress.media/?product=forged-in-fire

WIRED FOR SOUND
(Book Four of *The Mountaintop Series*)

Available from Amazon, Barnes & Noble and other Booksellers:

https://www.amazon.com/dp/B0CWZFVS5K

THE MOUNTAINTOP SERIES:

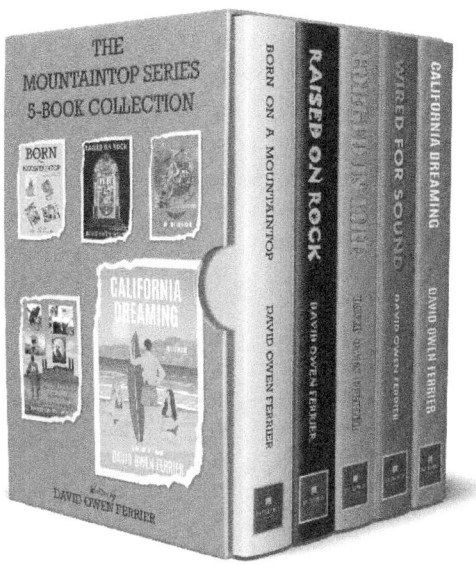

https://www.amazon.com/dp/B0CX25DQR7

Made in United States
North Haven, CT
28 August 2025

72242519R00176